Editor
Lorin E. Klistoff, M.A.

Editor in Chief
Karen J. Goldfluss, M.S. Ed.

Cover Artist
Marilyn Goldberg

Art Production Manager
Kevin Barnes

Imaging
Leonard P. Swierski

Publisher
Mary D. Smith, M.S. Ed.

VOCABULARY PUZZLES & ACTIVITIES

Building vocabulary skills one puzzle at a time!

Author

Nancy P. Sibtain

Teacher Created Resources, Inc.
6421 Industry Way
Westminster, CA 92683
www.teachercreated.com

ISBN: 978-1-4206-8076-8

© 2008 Teacher Created Resources, Inc.
Made in U.S.A.

Table of Contents

Table of Contents

# Introduction

Vocabulary Puzzles & Activities (Grade 4) is a challenging and fun way for children to improve their spelling, vocabulary, knowledge of synonyms, and grammar.

About the Book

The book is divided into three levels (Level A = Beginning, Level B = Intermediate, and Level C = Advanced). Students can, of course, move up or down the levels according to their needs. The clues of each crossword puzzle consist of three parts: the number of the square in which the word starts, the clue, and then a number in parentheses to tell the solver how many letters are in the solution word. (*Note:* If the number of letters shown in parentheses is, for example, (3, 3), it means that there are two words in the solution, each with three letters, e.g., "set off." The solution must be written in the crossword without a space between the words.)

Each crossword page also includes other activities to add to the enjoyment. The section "New words I have learned" gives students a space to write in unfamiliar words and reinforce their new vocabulary. Anagrams can be made by scrambling and rearranging the letters of a word to form another word or words (e.g., CANED is an anagram of DANCE). There are also activities that include hidden words, breaking codes, word searches, and much more!

In the back of the book, there is a word list that includes all the words used in the puzzles. Incorporate the words into your everyday classroom activities. For example, for each week, create a word list and activities from the words in a puzzle. Categorize by vowel sounds, syllabication rules, parts of speech, etc. Be creative!

Helpful Hints for Students

The best method for students to start a puzzle is to look through all the clues until they find one with a solution they know. This may be an across-word or a down-word. Once a student has written in the word in the correct space, the next step is to look at the clue for a word that crosses it, because one of the letters is given. Remind students that sometimes a word that seems to be the obvious and correct solution can turn out to be the wrong one. Also, encourage them to use the Internet as a resource when solving clues.

Let students know that when solving crossword puzzles, they do not need to start with the first clue. Sometimes two meanings, separated by a semicolon, are given in a clue to help the solver (e.g., Most plants have these; goes away from). A group of dashes is sometimes used in a clue where it is difficult to supply a synonym or other description. For example, the clue might be as follows: Dad picked me up from school in his – – – (3). The solution would be "car"—the number of dashes indicates the number of letters in the solution. An answer key for all puzzles is located on pages 56–61.

Tell students that it is important to carefully read the clue, especially in terms of the tense of the verb required. A clue that directs them to the word "saw" will clearly show that the past tense, not the present tense "see," is required. The same applies to the number. If the clue requires a plural word, a word in the singular will be the wrong word—even though it fits. For example, the clue might be as follows: Many people sit at these when they write (5). The solution will be "desks"; it could not be "table" because the clue asks for a plural word of five letters.

Have students use pencils for crossword-problem solving. Have them keep an eraser nearby, so they can easily erase an incorrect answer.

Overall, solving crossword puzzles is an enjoyable and stimulating activity that children can take with them into their adult lives. The completion of a puzzle can bring to child and adult alike that sense of achievement that we all need to experience from time to time. Good luck!

Name _____

Date _____

 **Unit 1**
(Answers on page 56)

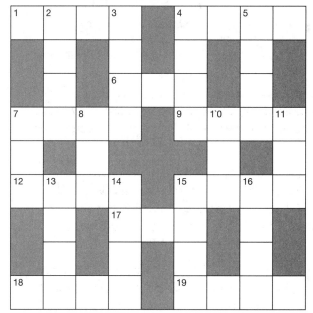

WORD LIST

ATE	LOG	PLAY	SENT
AWAY	LOSE	ROW	SHIN
BEAK	MILK	SAT	SWIM
BEES	NAIL	SAYS	TRAY
GOAT	NOSE	SEA	
HERO	OVAL	SEE	

Anagram

When we mix up the letters of a word, we can make a new word. This is called an ANAGRAM. For example, MEATS is an anagram of STEAM. Find a word in the crossword that is an anagram of TENS. (*Hint:* Write each letter on a separate paper and then rearrange them to make a word.)

_____

Across

1. The long bone in the front of my leg (4)
4. A bird uses this to pick up grain or insects (4)
6. Look at (3)
7. The opposite of win (4)
9. My teacher – – – – we must be quiet in class (4)
12. An animal with horns which is about the size of a sheep (4)
15. My aunt – – – – me a birthday card by e-mail (4)
17. We use oars when we – – – a boat (3)
18. Have fun with our friends (4)
19. A white drink which is also a food (4)

Down

2. Someone who does something brave or heroic (4)
3. We use this for the sense of smell (4)
4. Insects which make honey (4)
5. Not here; somewhere else (4)

7. We may put this piece of wood on the fire in winter (3)
8. A word similar to the meaning of "ocean" (3)
10. Consumed; had some food (3)
11. When the teacher said, "Sit" we all – – – down (3)
13. A curve that is egg-shaped (4)
14. When Mom has guests, she carries the drinks and food on this (4)
15. Move through the water by using arms and legs (4)
16. I have one of these at the end of each finger (4)

New words I have learned

_____

_____

_____

Name _____

Date _____

 Level A **Unit 2**

(Answers on page 56)

(Answers on page 56)

AFTER	GNAW	SCRUB
APE	HAS	SUN
BEAR	HUT	TEN
COW	KNEES	TWO
CRUMB	KNOW	WET
EATEN	LAMB	WRITE
EEL	LIE	

Hidden Word

Hidden words can run across two or more words (e.g., in the sentence "We went **to a st**reet party," the hidden word is "toast." Find the four-letter word in the Word List hidden in this sentence:

I WOULD LIKE TO BE A RADIO HOST.

_____

Across

1. A tiny bit of bread or cookie (5)
3. John – – – a cat with long whiskers (3)
5. Rainy; covered with water (3)
7. Dad picked me up – – – – – school (5)
8. I – – – – how to use a computer (4)
9. A young sheep (4)
12. Has my little sister – – – – – all the chocolates? (5)
14. A long fish that looks like a snake (3)
16. The star that warms the earth (3)
17. Put words on paper (5)

Down

1. An animal which gives milk (3)
2. An animal that sleeps for much of the winter (4)
3. A shelter or a simple house made of bark or wood (3)
4. Wash very hard, using a brush perhaps (5)
6. A low even number (3)
8. The joints which we use when we bend our legs (5)
10. A large animal such as a gorilla or chimpanzee (3)
11. This is what a dog does with a bone (4)
13. An even number between 7 and 15 (3)
15. Say something that is untrue (3)

Silent Letters

Write the six words in the Word List which have a silent letter (a letter we do not pronounce) at the beginning or end.

_____ _____ _____

_____ _____ _____

New words I have learned

_____

_____

Level A Unit 3
(Answers on page 56)

Find the Words

All the words in the Word List that begin with a <u>vowel</u> are hidden in the square. Can you find them?

F	N	O	P	A	S	M	I	L
P	O	S	L	E	A	G	E	R
Y	V	L	U	F	H	R	R	P
S	L	T	L	G	M	B	F	F
F	E	A	G	L	E	F	I	I
N	P	B	O	E	L	E	D	S
E	A	R	H	A	R	O	E	R
S	R	L	E	S	Y	N	A	U
F	I	D	V	Y	H	D	E	L

Across

1. Time can be divided into – – – – , present, and future (4)
5. Not difficult (4)
6. Mom will be very pleased that I – – – – – – the test (6)
8. A hot drink (3)
9. Wanting to do something badly (5)
10. We listen with this (3)
11. Repaired (something that was broken) (6)
12. We measure this in hours, days, weeks, years, and centuries (4)
13. A thought or suggestion which may pop into my mind (4)

Down

2. A boy and a girl in the same family are brother and – – – – – – (6)
3. A bright color (3)
4. A pharaoh (king) in ancient Egypt was buried in this (7)
6. Mothers and fathers (7)

7. A very big bird with strong wings (5)
8. A word meaning bought and sold or exchanged (6)
11. A sound made by a little kitten (3)

WORD LIST

EAGER	MEW	SISTER
EAGLE	PARENTS	TEA
EAR	PASSED	TIME
EASY	PAST	TRADED
IDEA	PYRAMID	
MENDED	RED	

New words I have learned

_____

_____

_____

 **Level A** ## Unit 4
(Answers on page 56)

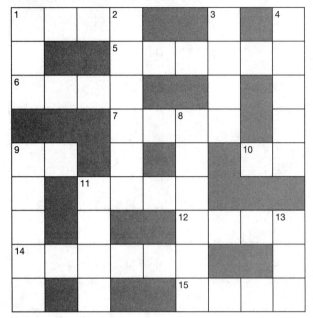

Words in Words

Remove the <u>first</u> letter or the <u>first two</u> letters from some words in the Word List, and you will discover other words.

_____ _____

_____ _____

_____ _____

Across

1. The amount we must pay for something we buy (4)
5. The way a person pronounces words; my aunt has a Scottish – – – – – – (6)
6. A small vessel with oars, a sail, or an engine (4)
7. Pulls quickly and sharply (4)
9. The opposite of come (2)
10. The opposite of down (2)
11. We may eat ice cream from this (4)
12. A notice in a shop showing us where to leave the building (4)
14. Frightened (6)
15. We may do this when we are tired or bored (4)

Down

1. A baby bear or baby lion (3)
2. A permanent picture or a word put onto the skin with a needle (6)
3. Not as much; a smaller quantity (4)
4. After a tree is cut down, this is what remains (5)

8. Wanting more than we can eat or more than we should have (6)
9. Very good; very big; The – – – – – Barrier Reef (5)
11. The inner part of an apple where the seeds are (4)
13. A silvery-white metal (3)

Hidden Words

In the following sentence, take a letter (in the same position) from each word to find the two hidden words.

BIG STORE STOPS ORDERING NEW FLOUR FOR CAKES.

_____ _____

New words I have learned

_____

_____

Name _____

Date _____

Unit 5
(Answers on page 56)

Anagram

If an E is added to a word in the Word List, the letters can be scrambled to make the anagram RODEOS. Which word?

_____

Hidden Words

Two of the words in the crossword are hidden in the following sentence. Remember that hidden words can run across two or more words.

WE MET SAM AT THE SHOPS, SO WE WALKED HOME TOGETHER.

_____ _____

Across

1 Dollars and cents (5)

3 A flower before it opens (3)

5 Move the head to show the answer is "yes" (3)

7 The opposite of tight (5)

9 A thick cloud of mist that may cover an area, especially on the mountains (3)

10 Twenty-four hours (3)

14 Jobs we must complete in school or at home (5)

15 Plant seeds in the ground; a mother pig (3)

16 We wipe our feet on this (3)

17 Falls; tiny bits of water (5)

Down

1 Gold, silver, or coal are dug out of this (4)

2 The yellow part of an egg (4)

4 An animal which has antlers (4)

6 We may open or close these when we go in or out of a room (5)

8 Gems found in Australia and put into rings or pendants (5)

11 The stalk of a flower (4)

12 Today I – – – – a brush to clean my shoes (4)

13 Mother sheep (*plural*) (4)

New words I have learned

_____

_____

_____

_____

Name _____

Date _____

 Level A **Unit 6**

(Answers on page 56)

Hidden Word

Take the third letter of each word in this sentence, and discover a word in the crossword that is spelled backwards.

MATTHEW HAS ANOTHER CAP.

_____

Which Word?

Which word in the Word List has all four points of the compass in it?

_____

Across

1. The eleventh month of the year (8)
6. A jewel such as a pearl, an opal, or a ruby (3)
7. Information about recent events (4)
9. The skin of an apple or an orange (4)
12. A pole set upright in the ground; I am on my way to – – – – this sign (4)
15. A plant in the garden which we don't want (4)
17. I still – – – my sister the two dollars that she lent me (3)
18. It – – – – – – – – began to rain, and we ran for shelter (8)

Down

2. An ugly monster in fairy stories (4)
3. We use these to make omelettes (4)
4. Dad has to bend over, so he won't – – – – his head (4)
5. Very strong cord used to tie a boat to the wharf (4)
7. A short sleep in the daytime (3)

8. James – – – almost late for school (3)
10. The night before, as in Christmas – – – (3)
11. The top of a container or box (3)
13. The big sticks used for rowing a boat (4)
14. We were – – – – to wait in the classroom (4)
15. At the end of the game, we – – – – quite tired (4)
16. Really, really bad; wicked (4)

New words I have learned

_____

_____

Name _____

Date _____

Unit 7

(Answers on page 56)

Anagram

One word in the crossword is an anagram of SHIPMATES. Which word?

_____

Across

1. Not brave or confident; rather frightened (5)
3. A ship at sea may send this three-letter signal to call for help (3)
5. A part of the mouth (3)
7. No longer fresh (e.g., bread) (5)
9. My brother had a tooth – – – – , so Mom took him to the dentist (4)
11. A ball game played on horseback (4)
12. The stalk of a flower (4)
14. An Australian word meaning friend or companion (4)
16. A command which must be obeyed (5)
18. When wood or paper is burned in a fire, this is what remains (3)
19. Finish; the last part (3)
20. A marsh; a place where the ground is very wet (5)

Down

1. We like to talk to our friends on this (9)
2. The name of this punctuation mark — ; run very fast for a short distance (4)
3. A word similar to the meaning of "ocean" (3)
4. A ship which is powered by steam (9)
6. A word meaning friend (3)
8. Tomorrow we are having a spelling – – – – (4)
10. The opposite of go (4)
13. A hot drink (3)
15. The upper limbs; a word meaning weapons (4)
17. Yesterday I – – – a lot of work to help my Dad (3)

New words I have learned

_____

_____

_____

Name _____

Date _____

Unit 8
(Answers on page 56)

Anagram

Which word in the crossword is an anagram of HEART ?

_____

Across

1. Have strong affection for; really enjoy (4)
5. Too; in addition to (4)
6. Boiled, fried, or baked (6)
8. It happened a long time – – – (3)
9. Mistake (5)
10. A group of things that belong together (3)
11. When we eat or drink, the food goes down this (6)
12. Close to (4)
13. My little sister – – – – lots of questions (4)

Down

2. A little flower; a bluish purple color (6)
3. The soft part under a dog's paw; a small block of writing paper (3)
4. A very large brown-skinned sphere from a palm tree (7)
6. Running after and trying to catch (7)
7. The name given to our planet (5)
8. These are used with bows to shoot at targets (6)
11. Make an attempt to do something (3)

New words I have learned

_____

_____

_____

Words from Words

How many words of three letters or more can you make from the letters of 2-down in the crossword? A score of five or more is good.

_____ _____

_____ _____

_____ _____

_____ _____

Name _____

Date _____

Level A # Unit 9

(Answers on page 57)

Word Pairs

Some words in the Word List can be put together in pairs. Find two pairs of words on the list which make sense when put together (e.g., FISH OIL).

_____ _____

_____ _____

Across

1. We buy things in this place (4)
4. An animal with fins (4)
6. Some people cook with electricity and some use this (3)
7. He was at home, but we – – – – not (4)
9. A place that is smaller than a city but bigger than a suburb (4)
12. A shelter we may use when camping (4)
15. Very pleased (4)
17. The organ of hearing (3)
18. Something that we see twinkling in the sky at night (4)
19. Part of a tree used for making furniture or for burning in a campfire (4)

Down

2. Enormous (4)
3. We turn this when we read a book (4)
4. A hand when closed very tightly is called this (4)
5. The opposite of quick or fast (4)
7. When we jump into the pool, we become – – – (3)
8. We do this in a race at a marathon (3)
10. We may use this for frying food (3)
11. A movement of the head meaning "yes" (3)
13. The sun rises in the – – – – ; the compass point opposite to the west (4)
14. Rip or pull apart (4)
15. Become bigger (4)
16. Another word for "too" (4)

Anagrams

Put these letters in the right order to make words from the Word List.

OWLS _____   ARE _____

SEAT _____

New words I have learned

_____

_____

Name _____

Date _____

 Level A

Unit 10
(Answers on page 57)

(Answers on page 57)

WORD LIST

ACTOR	FIB	PEACH
ALL	HAD	PIN
APPLE	HAY	PONY
ARMS	HOT	SCRUB
COIN	INDIA	TRAIN
ELF	LIP	TRY
EXIT	ONE	

Anagram

Find a word in the crossword which has the anagram CHEAP. _____

Across

1. A popular fruit; we are told that one of these a day keeps the doctor away! (5)
3. The opposite of cold (3)
5. A part of the mouth (3)
7. A country on the continent of Asia (5)
8. A small horse (4)
9. A small, flat piece of metal used as money (4)
12. Someone who performs on the stage, on TV, or in a film (5)
14. A small storybook character with pointed ears (3)
16. Dried grass used for animal food (3)
17. Clean by rubbing hard, perhaps with a brush (5)

Down

1. Everybody; the whole lot (3)
2. The way out of a building (4)
3. We – – – a great party (3)
4. Many people travel to school or to work on this (5)
6. A sharp little piece of metal used to hold material together when sewing (3)
8. A soft and juicy fruit (5)
10. Twelve minus eleven (3)
11. The upper limbs of the body (4)
13. Make an attempt (3)
15. A small but naughty lie (3)

Hidden Word

Find the word from the Word List hidden in this sentence. (Hidden words can run across two or more words; e.g., "I like to drin**k it ten** times each day"—the hidden word is "kitten.")

I PUT YOUR BOOK UP ON YOUR LOCKER.

_____

New words I have learned

_____

_____

Name _____

Date _____

Level A
Unit 11
(Answers on page 57)

(Answers on page 57)

1			2				3				4
						5				
6				7						
							8			
	9									
10										
			11							
12										
				13						

WORD LIST

ACORN   LOOSE   SEESAW
ANSWERS   LOW   SPIDERS
DOE   NEEDLE   USED
EVEN   OFF   WING
FEW   ONIONS
LEMONS   ROOF

Across

1. A bird and an airplane need two of this part to fly (4)
5. The opposite of odd numbers are called – – – – numbers (4)
6. Play equipment for two people which moves up and down (6)
8. A word opposite in meaning to high (3)
9. Not tight (5)
10. A mother deer (3)
11. Vegetables that can make your eyes water (6)
12. The very top part of a house (4)
13. When I spelled a word wrong, I – – – – an eraser to correct it (4)

Down

2. I use this when I sew (6)
3. Not many (3)
4. Replies (7)
6. Creatures with eight legs which make webs (7)
7. The smooth, hard fruit of the oak tree which squirrels love to eat (5)
8. These fruits are very sour (6)
11. The opposite of on (3)

Find the Words

Five words from the crossword have been hidden in this square. Can you find them?

R	N	O	P	U	S	M	I	L
S	E	E	S	A	W	O	R	U
P	V	L	U	C	H	R	R	K
I	L	T	L	O	M	B	O	F
D	E	S	P	R	I	F	O	I
E	P	B	O	N	L	E	F	S
R	Q	U	Y	U	P	O	R	R
S	R	L	E	M	O	N	S	U
F	I	D	V	Y	H	D	E	L

New words I have learned

_____

_____

_____

             #8076 Vocabulary Puzzles & Activities

Level A

Unit 12
(Answers on page 57)

Across

1. The largest continent, with many countries including India, China, and Japan (4)
5. A precious metal (6)
6. Very, very bad (4)
7. And they all lived happily – – – – after (4)
9. Little word meaning "therefore" (2)
10. This – – that? (2)
11. A small mark or a good name for a dog (4)
12. The side of a shape (4)
14. We go to this person when we are sick (6)
15. Something that we like to sing (4)

Down

1. A large type of monkey (3)
2. Not awake (6)
3. Above (4)
4. A mistake (5)
8. Comes into (6)
9. My cousin always – – – – – me a birthday card (5)
11. A very big bag used for carrying lots of potatoes (4)
13. We may eat this fried or scrambled (3)

WORD LIST

APE	ENTERS	SACK
ASIA	ERROR	SENDS
ASLEEP	EVER	SILVER
DOCTOR	EVIL	SO
EDGE	OR	SONG
EGG	OVER	SPOT

Which Word?

Take away the first letter of one word in the Word List to make a word which means FINISHES. Write the word from the Word List and the new word.

_____ _____

Anagram

Which word in the Word List is an anagram of LIVERS ?

_____

Choose a word on the Word List and mix up the letters to make an anagram. See if someone else can unscramble the letters and find the word.

_____

New words I have learned

_____

_____

_____

Name _____

Date _____

Unit 13

Level A

(Answers on page 57)

BIRD	FIX	MAY
BRAVE	GEESE	OGRE
BREAD	KEY	RIB
DAMP	KNIFE	STICK
DECK	LET	TOSS
EWE	MASTS	TYPE

Across

1. An important food we use to make sandwiches and toast (5)
3. Allow; permit (3)
5. One of the bones in your chest (3)
7. The tall posts on sailing boats to which the sails are attached (5)
9. One month of the year (3)
10. Mend; put right (3)
14. Farmyard birds (5)
15. We lock or unlock the door with this (3)
16. Mother sheep (3)
17. We can cut things with this (5)

Down

1. An animal with feathers (4)
2. A bit wet; moist (4)
4. Throw, without using much force (4)
6. Showing courage (5)
8. A little bit of wood from a tree (5)
11. A nasty, ugly giant in fairy tales (4)
12. The floor of a ship (4)
13. Write words using a computer keyboard (4)

Anagram

A verb is a "doing" word (like "run," "give," or "laugh"). But A VERB is also an anagram of one of the words in the crossword. Which word?

_____

Hidden Words

Two of the words in the crossword are hidden in the following sentence. Remember that hidden words can run across two or more words.

AT HOME WE FLY OUR PLASTIC KITE.

_____ _____

New words I have learned

_____

_____

_____

_____

Name _____

Date _____

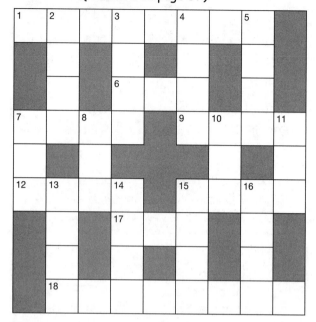

WORD LIST

APE	OBEY	SLOW
APRICOTS	OVAL	TAP
EEL	PEAR	TERM
ICE	PEST	TOE
INTO	PLAN	TRIO
LEMONADE	POET	YAWN
NUT	SAND	

Hidden Word

Take the third letter of each word in this sentence and discover a word in the crossword:

MATTHEW BORROWED BRIAN'S STOOL.

_____

Across

1. Soft fruit that look like small peaches (8)
6. This is at the end of my foot (3)
7. A group of three singers or musicians (4)
9. We sometimes do this when we are very tired or bored (4)
12. Person who writes poetry (4)
15. Nuisance; harmful insect (4)
17. A long fish that looks rather like a snake (3)
18. A refreshing drink (8)

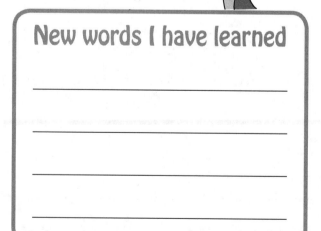

New words I have learned

_____

_____

_____

Down

2. A fruit that is wide at one end and narrow near the stalk (4)
3. Tom came – – – – the classroom when the teacher called him (4)
4. Do what we are told to do (4)
5. The opposite of quick (4)
7. Knock lightly (3)
8. Frozen water (3)
10. A large monkey (3)
11. An almond or walnut (3)
13. Something that is egg-shaped (4)
14. A section of the school year in Australia (4)
15. This may be drawn by an architect (4)
16. Fine particles of rock on the seashore (4)

Anagram

Find the word in the crossword which has the anagram ONE MEDAL.

_____

Name _____

Date _____

WORD LIST

AGED	IDLE	SAD
ALSO	LAKE	SIX
ART	NET	TOO
CAVE	NEW	VASE
DANGEROUS	OVER	VIXEN
EAT	PANDA	WAS
ELVES	PANIC	
GOOD	PINEAPPLE	

Anagram

If we rearrange all the letters of 4-down in the crossword, we can make the anagram A RUDE SONG! Test this by writing out the letters and then crossing them off to see if they spell the solution word for 4-down.

_____

Across

1. A sudden fear that some people suffer when they have to do something difficult (5)
3. Unhappy (3)
5. Not previously seen or used (3)
7. A female fox (5)
9. Very old (4)
11. I write stories, and I – – – – draw pictures (4)
12. A large area of water surrounded by land (4)
14. Above (4)
16. An animal that lives in the bamboo forests of China (5)
18. A word with the same meaning as the answer to 11-across in this puzzle (3)
19. Put in the mouth, chew, and swallow (3)
20. "The – – – – – and the Shoemaker" is a fairy tale story (5)

Down

1. A large, tropical fruit with a very thick, rough skin (9)
2. A hollow in a hill or mountain providing shelter from the weather (4)
3. A number higher than four and lower than ten (3)
4. Likely to cause harm or injury (9)
6. I ran because I – – – late for school (3)
8. Having nothing to do (4)
10. The opposite of bad (4)
13. Drawing or painting pictures (3)
15. We put cut flowers in this (4)
17. Material used for catching fish or keeping the mosquitoes out (3)

New words I have learned

_____

_____

_____

Name _____

Date _____

 Level A **Unit 16**
(Answers on page 57)

Across

1. Young bears (4)
5. A solid shape with six square faces (4)
6. We may use this to cross over a river (6)
8. Come first in a contest (3)
9. Remain in one place in the air as a helicopter can (5)
10. A tiny insect (3)
11. Brings together for a special purpose (6)
12. Requests (4)
13. Not tied up or locked up (4)

Down

2. Clever; shining (6)
3. Frozen water (3)
4. Shelters for dogs (7)
6. Soft pieces of fruit which are easy to peel; monkeys love to eat them (7)
7. This watch was – – – – – to me for my birthday (5)
8. The person who wrote the book; author (6)
11. I – – – a pencil to do my school work (3)

Which Word?

A Take away the first letter of one of the words in the crossword and the answer is a word meaning CORRECT. Write the word from the crossword and the new word.

_____ _____

B Take away the last letter of one of the words in the crossword and the answer is a word meaning YOU AND ME. Write both words.

_____ _____

New words I have learned

_____

_____

_____

_____

Name _____

Date _____

Level B **Unit 17**
(Answers on page 58)

Words in Words

Write the words in the Word List which have the following words in them (for example, AS is in FAST).

ONE _____ NOT _____

GET _____ CENT _____

ABLE _____ US _____

Across

1. A faint smell; a perfume (5)
4. Quick or quickly (4)
6. An organ in my chest which I use when I breathe (4)
7. When I got up, Dad had already – – – – to work (4)
9. A very short letter I might write to my friend (4)
11. The person who uses something (4)
12. A tiny particle of anything (4)
13. Without any hair (4)
14. We all know the – – – – about crossing the road (4)
15. A sauce which is served with a baked meat dish (5)

Down

1. A tiny piece of wood which may get into my finger (8)
2. A lump of gold or other precious metal (6)
3. These are held when shops sell their goods at reduced prices (5)
5. The day before Friday (8)
8. Another term for a numeral (6)
10. We may sit at this to have a meal or to do our homework (5)

Hidden Message

The code in this message can be broken if you replace each <u>vowel</u> with the vowel that comes <u>before</u> it alphabetically (for example, each "e" should be read as an "a," and so on).

ENYUNI WHU CEN RIED THOS MISSEGI OS VIRY CLIVIR

_____

_____

New words I have learned

_____

_____

Name _____

Date _____

Level B **Unit 18**
(Answers on page 58)

WORD LIST

BOOKS	OIL	REPLY
BROWN	PAPER	ROSES
CONCERT	PENCILS	SIDES
EVERY	PETER	STEPS
ICE	PROBLEM	SWIMS
INITIAL	RACES	TIN
NAMES	RAINY	WATER
NOD	RELAY	WRITE

Hidden Words

Two of the words in the crossword are hidden in this sentence. Remember that all punctuation should be ignored!

MY WALLET HAD FIVE DOLLARS IN IT; I ALMOST LEFT IT IN THE SHOP.

_____ _____

Anagrams

Find the word in the crossword that has the anagram SCARE. Make another five-letter word from the same letters.

_____ _____

Across

1. We write on this (5)
4. A dark color made by mixing red, yellow, and blue (5)
7. A silvery-white metal (3)
8. Something that must be solved; something difficult (7)
9. In – – – – – weather we need an umbrella (5)
10. Moves through the water using arms and legs (5)
12. Flowers that usually have thorns on their stems (5)
14. Put words on paper (5)
16. A musical performance where people play or sing (7)
18. Frozen water (3)
19. The edges of a thing; there are two – – – – – to every argument (5)
20. A race in which teams of runners compete (5)

5. Mom uses this when she fries the potatoes (3)
6. We wrote our – – – – – on the birthday card (5)
11. My name is Emma and my – – – – – – – is "E" (7)
12. Running, swimming, or riding competitions (5)
13. When a baby starts walking, we say he takes his first – – – – – (5)
14. The precious liquid in the seas and rivers; H_2O (5)
15. Each; – – – – – one (5)
17. Move the head to show that you agree (3)

Down

1. The name of a mischievous rabbit in a story by Beatrix Potter (5)
2. I write and draw with these (7)
3. Answer (5)
4. We read these (5)

New words I have learned

_____

_____

Name _____

Date _____

 Level B # Unit 19
(Answers on page 58)

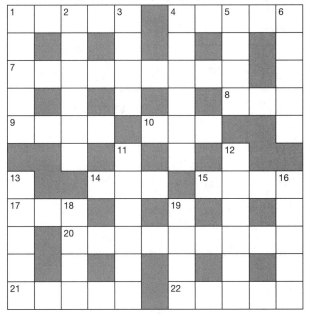

Across

1. The opposite of light (in weight) (5)
4. An Australian animal whose diet is eucalyptus leaves (5)
7. These insects try to bite us at night (9)
8. Acorns grow on this tree (3)
9. A small building near the house where tools or other things are stored (4)
10. Tiny drops of water that cover the ground at night (3)
14. Mend; put right (3)
15. A movie; something that is put into a camera (4)
17. I like to – – – on the couch and read a book (3)
20. Went on and on without stopping (9)
21. Grain which has been ground and is used in cakes (5)
22. A tortoise has this on its back (5)

Down

1. Camels have these (5)
2. Reply (6)
3. Belonging to you (4)
4. A baby cat (6)
5. Too; as well (4)

Find the Words

The six four-letter words in the crossword are hidden in this square.

P	R	A	L	S	O	F	K	M
L	E	M	I	I	N	E	L	Y
O	B	E	S	L	A	C	N	T
N	N	O	L	T	V	H	U	S
F	I	L	M	F	T	O	L	Y
S	M	P	R	I	N	A	C	O
H	A	L	S	N	U	M	D	U
E	R	N	Y	S	N	P	E	R
D	I	G	O	V	E	S	E	R

6. The opposite of asleep (5)
11. A meal usually eaten in the evening (6)
12. There are sixty seconds in this (6)
13. The edge of steep rocks near the sea (5)
16. A prize awarded at the Olympic Games (5)
18. The sound of my voice coming back to me (4)
19. When fish swim, they use these to help them to move along (4)

New words I have learned

_____

_____

Name _____

Date _____

 Level B **Unit 20**
(Answers on page 58)

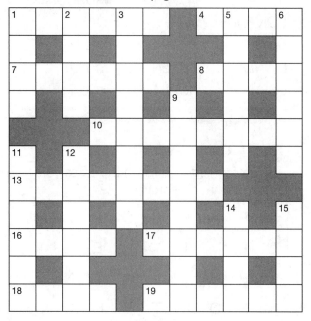

This crossword is about writing. See if you can follow the story and fill in the correct spaces in the crossword. You will need to count the number of letters in the space before you write in a word. If you are not sure about a word, leave it and come back to it later.

These days, it is so easy to use (1-across) to talk to your friends. But sometimes it is nice to write a (6-down) in order to (7-across) an invitation or tell a friend about some special (1-down) that you have in mind. If you are using a (17-across) and you make a mistake, the wrong word can be (12-down) with an eraser. A (6-down) always (18-across) with words such as "Yours sincerely," "Love," or "From," followed by your name. When you have finished writing, you must put the (6-down) into an (10-across) and (4-across) the (15-down); then put a stamp on it and take it to a mailbox. While you are (19-across), the letter sorters in the post office will prepare your letter for delivery.

One type of person who uses a pen or (17-across) all the time is an (5-down) who (13-across) books and stories in newspapers before they are published. Moms and dads often need to write a (8-across) of their

WORD LIST

ACCEPT	ERASED	PENCIL
ACHE	EXPENSES	PHONES
ASLEEP	FEATHERS	PLAN
CORRECTS	FLAP	RUSH
EDITOR	LETTER	SCARCE
ENDS	LIST	SEAL
ENVELOPE	ONCE	

household (3-down) and write checks to pay the bills.

(2-down) upon a time [a long time ago], those who knew how to write were very (11-down) [there were very few of them]. In ancient Egypt, for example, (6-down)-writers, called scribes, would write for other people. They had to do a lot of (6-down)-writing and it is likely that their hands would sometimes (14-down).

Before modern pens were invented, people used to write with quills which were made from (9-down). The hard ends of these were cut to make points. The writer would hold the quill pen in the way that we hold a (17-across) and would dip the point into ink. Later came steel nibs, fountain pens, and ballpoints.

Most people today spend a lot of time using computers, but it is important that we continue to use a pen or a (17-across) and paper and try to write clearly and neatly. We must never write badly just because we are trying to (16-across) our work and finish quickly. Good handwriting is very important in our class work and homework.

New words I have learned

_____

_____

_____

Name _____

Date _____

Level B **Unit 21**
(Answers on page 58)

Words from Words

How many words of three letters or more can you make from 13-across in the crossword? A score of five is good.

_____ _____
_____ _____
_____ _____
_____ _____

Across

1. A person who rides a horse in a horse race (6)
3. To decorate with; e.g., – – – – the Christmas tree (4)
7. A dietitian advises us about this (4)
8. People in circuses who make us laugh (6)
10. People who correct books and newspaper articles before they are published (7)
11. People who organize parties want everyone to be happy and to have – – – (3)
12. People who work in coal mines go down into this deep, dark hole (3)
13. People who make men's suits and other garments (7)
15. The person in charge of a reptile park will certainly have this reptile (6)
17. Some music teachers teach pupils to – – – – songs (4)
18. Every worker uses some kind of – – – – (4)
19. A person whose job used to be to make the king laugh (6)

Down

1. The person who makes the decision in a law court or in a competition (5)
2. A person who makes medicines; a pharmacist (7)
4. Use oars on a boat (3)
5. A person who makes things out of stone is called a stone – – – – – (5)
6. A dressmaker may use this stretchy material to make waistbands (7)
9. The people we visit when we are sick (7)
11. The person who sells flowers (7)
12. The person who flies an airplane or helicopter (5)
14. People called cane growers provide us with this sweet stuff (5)
16. A person who looks after animals may work in this place (3)

New words I have learned

_____

_____

Name _____

Date _____

Level B Unit 22
(Answers on page 58)

Anagram

Find the word in the crossword that has the anagram LEAD OWL.

_____

Words in Words

Write the words from the crossword which have the following words in them, with the letters in the correct order.

A BIT_____   E LOW_____

B HEAP_____   F RAKE_____

C INK_____   G RUB_____

D LIT_____   H THIN_____

Across

1. The loops in a chain (5)
4. Something we do without thinking much about it; it may be good or bad (5)
7. Two is – – – equal to three (3)
8. People who make sure that the rules are obeyed in a sports match; referees (7)
9. Loud, unpleasant sound (5)
10. A father duck (5)
12. A large, striped cat in Asia (5)
14. Come apart; break or divide into parts (5)
16. Less expensive (7)
18. This is woven by a spider (3)
19. Firm; not hollow (5)
20. I might wear this to show that I belong to a club or group (5)

Down

1. Tablecloths may be made of this material woven from flax (5)
2. Not anything (7)
3. We may add this liquid to our food to improve the flavor (5)
4. Expected or wanted something to happen (5)
5. A long piece of wood or metal; a – – – of chocolate (3)
6. The one of our five senses which involves the tongue (5)
11. Permitted (to do something) (7)
12. Short, sharp little pins or nails (5)
13. Very fast (5)
14. Clean by rubbing very hard, perhaps using a brush (5)
15. We sit at this to eat or do our homework (5)
17. A snake-like fish (3)

New words I have learned

_____

_____

Level B — Unit 26
(Answers on page 59)

(crossword grid with numbered cells: 2, 3, 4, 5, 6, 8, 10, 11, 12, 14, 15, 16, 18, 19, 20, 22)

Across
1. Cannot be bent or forced out of shape (5)
4. This tells us the time (5)
7. Vehicle which takes very sick patients to hospital (9)
8. I do – – – want to be late for school (3)
9. The handle of a sword (4)
10. The opposite of good (3)
14. A large hole in the ground; a word often used to mean a coal mine (3)
15. The sister of my father or mother is my – – – – (4)
17. A word which joins words or parts of sentences (3)
20. These happen by chance and sometimes result in people being hurt (9)
21. A popular fruit (5)
22. A book of maps (5)

Down
1. Arrive at; stretch out the arm to take something (5)
2. Eat quickly and noisily (6)
3. Not shiny; not very interesting (4)

WORD LIST

ACCIDENTS	CIRCLE	NOT
AMBULANCE	CLOCK	OVEN
AND	DAMP	PANDA
APPLE	DULL	PIT
ATLAS	GOBBLE	REACH
AUNT	HILT	RIGID
BAD	IDEA	TASKS
CANVAS	KNOTS	TUNNEL

Find the Words

The six <u>four-letter words</u> in the crossword are hidden in this square.

P	R	E	L	H	O	F	K	M
L	E	M	I	I	N	R	L	Y
O	B	E	S	L	A	U	N	T
N	N	O	L	T	V	N	U	S
I	D	E	A	F	T	D	L	L
V	M	P	R	I	N	A	C	K
U	D	U	L	L	U	M	D	R
S	R	N	Y	I	N	P	E	R
T	I	G	O	V	E	N	E	R

4. A rough cloth used to make sails and tents (6)
5. The place in which food is baked (4)
6. We make these when we tie pieces of string together (5)
11. A round plane figure shaped like a ring or a dinner plate (6)
12. An underground passage built for trains, etc. (6)
13. A large animal like a bear which eats bamboo (5)
16. Jobs which must be done (5)
18. Moist; slightly wet (4)
19. A thought or a plan which may pop into my head (4)

Level B — Unit 23
(Answers on page 58)

(crossword grid with numbered cells: 1, 2, 3, 4, 5, 6, 7, 8, 9, 10, 11, 12, 13, 14, 15, 16, 17, 18, 19, 20, 21, 22)

Across
1. The third month of the year (5)
4. A machine that can be programmed to perform tasks usually done by people (5)
7. The ninth month of the year (9)
8. Resting place for a lion or a bear (3)
9. Genuine; not imaginary (4)
10. My dog, cat, hamster, or goldfish (3)
14. I can wave this to cool myself (3)
15. Seize suddenly and roughly (4)
17. Jump up and down on one foot (3)
20. Unfortunate and unexpected events (9)
21. Go into a room or hall (5)
22. When we walk, we take long or short – – – – – (5)

New words I have learned

_____

_____

WORD LIST

ACCIDENTS	HEEL	REPEAT
ADDS	HOP	ROBBER
BIRD	MARCH	ROBOT
BUSES	MISER	SAUCER
DEN	ORANGE	SEPTEMBER
ENTER	PAST	STEPS
FAN	PET	TWINS
GRAB	REAL	WHOLE

Hidden Words

Four words from the crossword are hidden in this sentence.

<u>THE CHILDREN IN THE SHOP WERE ALL FROM OUR SCHOOL. THOSE WHO LEFT WITH US TOOK THE ELEVATOR TO THE GROUND FLOOR.</u>

_____ _____

_____ _____

Down
1. A person who has lots of money but doesn't want to spend it (5)
2. Do or say (something) more than once (6)
3. The back part of a foot (4)
4. Some one who steals (6)
5. An animal that lays eggs and can fly (4)
6. Two children of the same family born on the same day and year (5)
11. A cup is put on this (6)
12. A fruit and a color (6)
13. Two halves or four quarters make this (5)
16. Big vehicles in which we may travel to and from school (5)
18. Time can be divided into – – – –, present, and future (4)
19. Puts numbers together to find the total (4)

Level B

Unit 24
(Answers on page 58)

Across

1. The amount of turn between two lines which meet at a point (5)
4. Another word for a mathematical symbol (4)
6. When we owe money, we say we are in – – – – (4)
7. Go upwards (4)
9. One of the small slabs on the bathroom floor (4)
11. The opposite of false (4)
12. A word sometimes used in poetry to mean island (4)
13. The amount of space a flat surface takes up (4)
14. Require (4)
15. When the wood has been burned, we are left with – – – – – (5)

Anagram

Which word in the crossword is an anagram of I DREW ?

WORD LIST

ADDITION	ISLE	STEALS
ANGLE	LINES	TILE
AREA	NEED	TRES
ASHES	NUMERALS	TRUE
DEBT	RISE	WIDER
GAB	SIGN	

Backward Words

Some words have smaller words in them spelled backwards; e.g. the word FUR**NAC**E contains CAN spelled backwards. Find the words on the Word List that contain the following words spelled backwards:

Ⓐ ARE _____

Ⓑ BED _____   Ⓔ NIL _____

Ⓒ ERA _____   Ⓕ RED _____

Ⓓ LIT _____   Ⓖ SIR _____

Down

1. The act of putting numbers together to make a total (8)
2. To talk thoughtlessly or fast (3)
3. Of greater size when measured from side to side (5)
5. Figures we use to represent numbers (8)
8. Takes away, not mathematically but unlawfully; a robber does this (6)
10. To make these straight, we use a ruler (5)
16. The number "3" in Spanish (4)

New words I have learned

_____

_____

_____

Level B

Unit 25
(Answers on page 59)

Across

1. A food made in a bakery (5)
4. These must be tied when we put on our shoes (5)
7. A word meaning how old you are (3)
8. Baked in an oven or on an open fire (7)
9. Bright; reflects light (5)
10. When we sing a song, we must sing the right – – – – – (5)
12. Started (5)
14. The old name for this was "wireless" (5)
16. This is empty; there is – – – – – – – in it (7)
18. When we take six away from seven, this remains (3)
19. A tool for digging (5)
20. Very big plants with tall trunks (5)

WORD LIST

AGE	LACES	RIGH
BANKS	LEARN	ROAS
BEADS	NOISE	SHINY
BEGAN	NOTES	SIDES
BREAD	NOTHING	SPAD
CAT	ONE	TADP
DIRTY	OVENS	TEA
EVENING	RADIO	TREE

Anagram

Find the word in the crossword that the anagram NO NIGHT.

_____

Hidden Word

Take the last letter of each word to word in the crossword.

ROLL THE UMBRELLA FOR JOHN

Down

1. These can be put on a string to ma necklace (5)
2. The time between the afternoon an night (7)
3. Not clean; grubby (5)
4. At school we – – – – to read and v
5. A furry household pet (3)
6. Squares and rectangles have four c
11. This little swimmer will turn into a fr
12. Places which take care of people's
13. A loud sound which may not be ve
14. The opposite of left or wrong (5)
15. Cakes are baked in these (5)
17. A hot drink (3)

New words I have lear

_____

Name _____

Date _____

 Level B # Unit 27
(Answers on page 59)

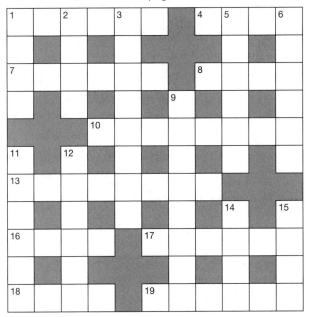

Which Word?

Take away the first letter from a word in the crossword to find a word which means "belonging to us."

_____

Across

1. The person who brings our food in a restaurant (6)
4. Twelve divided by three (4)
7. We can wash ourselves under this (6)
8. Quickly (4)
10. Our parents tell us not to talk to or accept a ride from this person (8)
13. People who take care of our teeth (8)
16. Something that may pop into your mind to solve a problem (4)
17. Large area of wilderness with tall trees (6)
18. At the end of the path, there is a – – – – to open (4)
19. Not awake (6)

Down

1. Make ourselves or our clothes clean (4)
2. We use this to make our clothes smooth (4)
3. If a heater is not powered by gas, it must be – – – – – – – – (8)
5. This juicy fruit is also the name of a color (6)
6. Come back (6)
9. Funny drawings which tell stories in magazines or on television (8)
11. We are doing this when we say that six plus six equals twelve (6)
12. Any small creature with six legs (6)
14. In this place (4)
15. Halt; don't go any further (4)

Anagram

Find a word in the crossword which has the anagram GO NEAR.

_____

New words I have learned

_____

_____

Name _____

Date _____

Level B **Unit 28**
(Answers on page 59)

Hidden Word

Find a word in the crossword by taking the third letter of each word in this sentence.

HURRY, THE SWEETS WILL DISAPPEAR!

_____

Across

1. The mass or heaviness of something (6)
3. Cover or enclose in paper or soft material (4)
7. To not succeed or pass; I don't want to – – – – this test (4)
8. A hot powder used to flavor food (6)
10. Causes; explanations given for doing something (7)
11. A stove or a heater may be powered by this; Oxygen is a – – – (3)
12. To say something which is totally untrue (3)
13. Not as old as someone else (7)
15. A very heavy object used to stop the ship moving (6)
17. The words which help you to put the right word in a crossword; this is one (4)
18. Very narrow strip used for fastening things. Sticky – – – – (4)
19. People who are invited to visit our homes (6)

Down

1. A very thin, crisp cookie (5)
2. Copy (7)
4. Tear roughly (3)
5. The capital city of France (5)
6. A temperature scale. It is 23 degrees – – – – – – – (7)
9. Any plane figure with three or more angles and straight sides (7)
11. Divers wear these to keep the water from their eyes (7)
12. The smallest amount (5)
14. Cylinders on which film or fishing line may be wound (5)
16. Something which usually has a saucer (3)

New words I have learned

_____

_____

Name _____

Date _____

Level B **Unit 23**

(Answers on page 58)

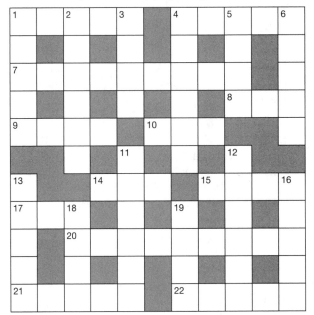

(Answers on page 58)

WORD LIST

ACCIDENTS	HEEL	REPEAT
ADDS	HOP	ROBBER
BIRD	MARCH	ROBOT
BUSES	MISER	SAUCER
DEN	ORANGE	SEPTEMBER
ENTER	PAST	STEPS
FAN	PET	TWINS
GRAB	REAL	WHOLE

Hidden Words

Four words from the crossword are hidden in this sentence.

THE CHILDREN IN THE SHOP WERE ALL FROM OUR SCHOOL. THOSE WHO LEFT WITH US TOOK THE ELEVATOR TO THE GROUND FLOOR.

_____ _____

_____ _____

Across

1. The third month of the year (5)
4. A machine that can be programmed to perform tasks usually done by people (5)
7. The ninth month of the year (9)
8. Resting place for a lion or a bear (3)
9. Genuine; not imaginary (4)
10. My dog, cat, hamster, or goldfish (3)
14. I can wave this to cool myself (3)
15. Seize suddenly and roughly (4)
17. Jump up and down on one foot (3)
20. Unfortunate and unexpected events (9)
21. Go into a room or hall (5)
22. When we walk, we take long or short – – – – – (5)

Down

1. A person who has lots of money but doesn't want to spend it (5)
2. Do or say (something) more than once (6)
3. The back part of a foot (4)
4. Some one who steals (6)
5. An animal that lays eggs and can fly (4)
6. Two children of the same family born on the same day and year (5)
11. A cup is put on this (6)
12. A fruit and a color (6)
13. Two halves or four quarters make this (5)
16. Big vehicles in which we may travel to and from school (5)
18. Time can be divided into – – – – , present, and future (4)
19. Puts numbers together to find the total (4)

New words I have learned

_____

_____

Name _____

Date _____

Level B # Unit 24
(Answers on page 58)

Across

1. The amount of turn between two lines which meet at a point (5)
4. Another word for a mathematical symbol (4)
6. When we owe money, we say we are in – – – – (4)
7. Go upwards (4)
9. One of the small slabs on the bathroom floor (4)
11. The opposite of false (4)
12. A word sometimes used in poetry to mean island (4)
13. The amount of space a flat surface takes up (4)
14. Require (4)
15. When the wood has been burned, we are left with – – – – – (5)

Backward Words

Some words have smaller words in them spelled backwards; e.g. the word FUR**NAC**E contains CAN spelled backwards. Find the words on the Word List that contain the following words spelled backwards:

A) ARE _____

B) BED _____   E) NIL _____

C) ERA _____   F) RED _____

D) LIT _____   G) SIR _____

Down

1. The act of putting numbers together to make a total (8)
2. To talk thoughtlessly or fast (3)
3. Of greater size when measured from side to side (5)
5. Figures we use to represent numbers (8)
8. Takes away, not mathematically but unlawfully; a robber does this (6)
10. To make these straight, we use a ruler (5)
16. The number "3" in Spanish (4)

Anagram

Which word in the crossword is an anagram of I DREW ?

_____

New words I have learned

_____

_____

_____

Name _____

Date _____

Anagram

Find the word in the crossword that has the anagram NO NIGHT.

_____

Hidden Word

Take the last letter of each word to find a word in the crossword.

ROLL THE UMBRELLA FOR JOHN.

_____

Across

1. A food made in a bakery (5)
4. These must be tied when we put on our shoes (5)
7. A word meaning how old you are (3)
8. Baked in an oven or on an open fire (7)
9. Bright; reflects light (5)
10. When we sing a song, we must sing the right — — — — — (5)
12. Started (5)
14. The old name for this was "wireless" (5)
16. This is empty; there is — — — — — — — in it (7)
18. When we take six away from seven, this remains (3)
19. A tool for digging (5)
20. Very big plants with tall trunks (5)

Down

1. These can be put on a string to make a necklace (5)
2. The time between the afternoon and the night (7)
3. Not clean; grubby (5)
4. At school we — — — — — to read and write (5)
5. A furry household pet (3)
6. Squares and rectangles have four of these (5)
11. This little swimmer will turn into a frog (7)
12. Places which take care of people's money (5)
13. A loud sound which may not be very nice (5)
14. The opposite of left or wrong (5)
15. Cakes are baked in these (5)
17. A hot drink (3)

New words I have learned

_____

_____

Name _____

Date _____

 Level B # Unit 26
(Answers on page 59)

1		2		3		4		5		6
7									
						8			
9				10					
			11				12		
13		14			15		16		
17		18			19				
	20								
21					22				

Across

1. Cannot be bent or forced out of shape (5)
4. This tells us the time (5)
7. Vehicle which takes very sick patients to hospital (9)
8. I do – – – want to be late for school (3)
9. The handle of a sword (4)
10. The opposite of good (3)
14. A large hole in the ground; a word often used to mean a coal mine (3)
15. The sister of my father or mother is my – – – – (4)
17. A word which joins words or parts of sentences (3)
20. These happen by chance and sometimes result in people being hurt (9)
21. A popular fruit (5)
22. A book of maps (5)

Down

1. Arrive at; stretch out the arm to take something (5)
2. Eat quickly and noisily (6)
3. Not shiny; not very interesting (4)

WORD LIST

ACCIDENTS	CIRCLE	NOT
AMBULANCE	CLOCK	OVEN
AND	DAMP	PANDA
APPLE	DULL	PIT
ATLAS	GOBBLE	REACH
AUNT	HILT	RIGID
BAD	IDEA	TASKS
CANVAS	KNOTS	TUNNEL

Find the Words

The six <u>four-letter words</u> in the crossword are hidden in this square.

P	R	E	L	H	O	F	K	M
L	E	M	I	I	N	R	L	Y
O	B	E	S	L	A	U	N	T
N	N	O	L	T	V	N	U	S
I	D	E	A	F	T	D	L	L
V	M	P	R	I	N	A	C	K
U	D	U	L	L	U	M	D	R
S	R	N	Y	I	N	P	E	R
T	I	G	O	V	E	N	E	R

4. A rough cloth used to make sails and tents (6)
5. The place in which food is baked (4)
6. We make these when we tie pieces of string together (5)
11. A round plane figure shaped like a ring or a dinner plate (6)
12. An underground passage built for trains, etc. (6)
13. A large animal like a bear which eats bamboo (5)
16. Jobs which must be done (5)
18. Moist; slightly wet (4)
19. A thought or a plan which may pop into my head (4)

Name _____

Date _____

 Level B

Unit 27
(Answers on page 59)

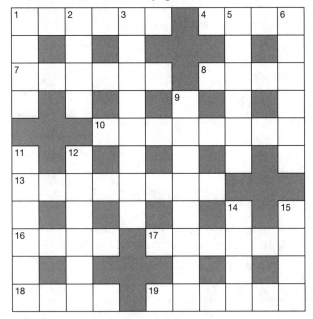

Which Word?

Take away the first letter from a word in the crossword to find a word which means "belonging to us."

_____

Across

1. The person who brings our food in a restaurant (6)
4. Twelve divided by three (4)
7. We can wash ourselves under this (6)
8. Quickly (4)
10. Our parents tell us not to talk to or accept a ride from this person (8)
13. People who take care of our teeth (8)
16. Something that may pop into your mind to solve a problem (4)
17. Large area of wilderness with tall trees (6)
18. At the end of the path, there is a – – – – to open (4)
19. Not awake (6)

Down

1. Make ourselves or our clothes clean (4)
2. We use this to make our clothes smooth (4)
3. If a heater is not powered by gas, it must be – – – – – – – – (8)
5. This juicy fruit is also the name of a color (6)
6. Come back (6)
9. Funny drawings which tell stories in magazines or on television (8)
11. We are doing this when we say that six plus six equals twelve (6)
12. Any small creature with six legs (6)
14. In this place (4)
15. Halt; don't go any further (4)

Anagram

Find a word in the crossword which has the anagram GO NEAR.

_____

New words I have learned

_____

_____

Name _____

Date _____

 Level B # Unit 28
(Answers on page 59)

Hidden Word

Find a word in the crossword by taking the third letter of each word in this sentence.

HURRY, THE SWEETS WILL DISAPPEAR!

_____

Across

1. The mass or heaviness of something (6)
3. Cover or enclose in paper or soft material (4)
7. To not succeed or pass; I don't want to – – – – this test (4)
8. A hot powder used to flavor food (6)
10. Causes; explanations given for doing something (7)
11. A stove or a heater may be powered by this; Oxygen is a – – – (3)
12. To say something which is totally untrue (3)
13. Not as old as someone else (7)
15. A very heavy object used to stop the ship moving (6)
17. The words which help you to put the right word in a crossword; this is one (4)
18. Very narrow strip used for fastening things. Sticky – – – – (4)
19. People who are invited to visit our homes (6)

Down

1. A very thin, crisp cookie (5)
2. Copy (7)
4. Tear roughly (3)
5. The capital city of France (5)
6. A temperature scale. It is 23 degrees – – – – – – – (7)
9. Any plane figure with three or more angles and straight sides (7)
11. Divers wear these to keep the water from their eyes (7)
12. The smallest amount (5)
14. Cylinders on which film or fishing line may be wound (5)
16. Something which usually has a saucer (3)

New words I have learned

_____

_____

Name _____

Date _____

 **Unit 29**
(Answers on page 59)

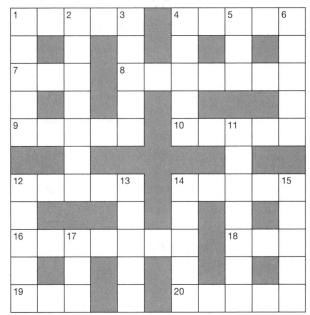

Words Inside Words

Write the words from the crossword which have the following words, in the correct order, <u>inside</u> them.

A ART _____

B BAN _____

C COT _____

D EAR _____

E EELS _____

F HAD _____

G ICE _____

H OWE _____

Across

1 Shelter from the sun (5)

4 In spelling, the letter A, E, I, O, or U (5)

7 The soft coat of a cat (3)

8 After it has rained, we may see this in the sky (7)

9 These keep the feet warm (5)

10 Go in or come in (5)

12 Make a change in something (5)

14 A group of grapes or flowers (5)

16 In science fiction, a being from the planet Mars (7)

18 Frozen water (3)

19 There are 2,000 pounds in this (5)

20 A fertile place in the desert (5)

Down

1 Strong cabinets where valuables are stored (5)

2 A yellowish fruit with a pit which looks like a small peach (7)

3 My sister – – – – – $40 each weekend as a babysitter (5)

4 We use this when we speak or sing (5)

5 A spider makes this (3)

6 Further down; not as high (5)

11 If we need to go to a hospital to have these removed, after the operation we get ice cream and other cold treats (7)

12 Confess; allow to enter (5)

13 Lift up (5)

14 A musical instrument similar to a guitar (5)

15 The back parts of our feet (5)

17 Move at a speed faster than a walk (3)

New words I have learned

_____

_____

_____

Name _____

Date _____

WORD LIST

ABOUT	MILL	THUMB
BABIES	OVER	TICKET
BAT	RAM	TIMES
BUS	RECTANGLE	TIRED
DIET	SHORT	TOTAL
HAT	SIGNAL	TRIANGLES
LEAP	SNOW	VIOLIN
LOSES	STEM	WINGS

Hidden Words

Two words from the crossword are hidden in this sentence. Ignore punctuation.

WE RAN ROUND THE TRACK AFTER TENNIS; NO WONDER WE WERE READY FOR A MILKSHAKE!

_____ _____

Across

1 The sum; the whole amount (5)

4 The opposite of long (5)

7 A four-sided figure with two pairs of parallel sides and four right angles (9)

8 A male sheep (3)

9 The kind of food that I normally eat. My uncle is on a – – – – to lose weight (4)

10 A baseball player hits the ball with this; an animal that sleeps upside down (3)

14 This is worn on the head (3)

15 A building with machinery for grinding grain (4)

17 Some people travel to school in this (3)

20 Figures with three straight sides and three angles (9)

21 Some– – – – I forget how to spell a word (5)

22 A bird uses these to fly (5)

Down

1 Weary; ready to have a rest or a sleep (5)

2 A person who wants to travel by train must first buy this (6)

3 Jump or spring a long way (4)

4 A light on the railway to warn or assist train drivers (6)

5 Above (4)

6 On each hand we have one (5)

11 Newly-born or very young children (6)

12 A string instrument played with a bow (6)

13 The story is – – – – – three little pigs (5)

16 Misplaces; doesn't win (5)

18 The stalk that supports the flower (4)

19 Frozen flakes that fall from the sky in very cold areas (4)

New words I have learned

_____

_____

_____

Name _____

Date _____

Unit 31

(Answers on page 59)

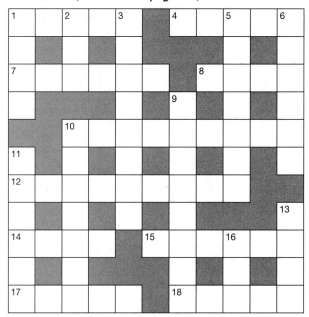

Anagram

Find the word in the crossword that has the anagram SEA DUTY.

_____

Hidden Word

Write down the third letter of each word in this sentence, and then read it from right to left. Write the new word on the line below.
FRED HELPS MOTHER CLEAR THE TABLE.

_____

Across

1. Seashore animals that run sideways (5)
4. A large Asian or African snake often used by snake charmers (5)
7. Tired and ready for bed (6)
8. To join two pieces of string together firmly, we must make this (4)
10. These are made by multiplying hundreds by tens (9)
12. Everybody asks these (9)
14. Puts numbers together to get a total (4)
15. Baby pig (6)
17. The country in which there are pyramids (5)
18. Very glad; joyful (5)

Down

1. When we buy something, we can pay for it by check, credit card, or – – – – (4)
2. A tool used to chop wood (3)
3. Gives help and encouragement to; Dad – – – – – – – – our local football team (8)
5. These are very easy to peel (7)

6. Someone who draws or paints pictures (6)
9. Surprise greatly; amaze (8)
10. Two days later than Sunday (7)
11. A figure with four equal sides and four right angles (6)
13. Remain; don't go away (4)
16. When I sit, my kitten wants to sit on my – – – (3)

New words I have learned

_____

_____

_____

_____

 **Unit 32**

Level C

(Answers on page 59)

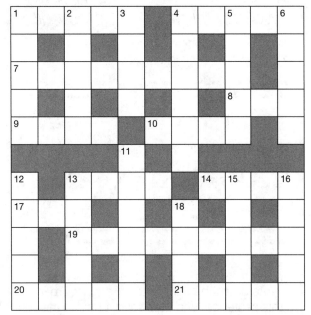

Words from Words

Make four words <u>of four letters or more</u> using letters from 7-across in the crossword.

_____ _____

_____ _____

Anagram

Find the word in the Word List which has the anagram SEEM MOIST.

_____

Across

1 These may be used on our doors to stop others from opening them (5)

4 We make toast from this (5)

7 A vehicle, with people in it, which travels to other planets (9)

8 Not the bottom, but the – – – (3)

9 This can be added to food to improve the flavor (4)

10 Jealousy; wanting something that someone else owns (4)

13 We say that a half-open door is – – – – (4)

14 Shut (a door) loudly and roughly (4)

17 We put this, and another one, on our feet to move on the snow (3)

19 Now and then; not very often (9)

20 A very long weapon with a pointed tip (5)

21 Stands up; ascends (5)

Down

1 Does not wear out; remains for a long time (5)

2 Move forward on hands and knees (5)

3 This is put in the soil and a plant grows from it (4)

4 The opposite of "in front of" (6)

5 With nothing in it (5)

6 Water is wasted when a faucet does this (5)

11 A person who owns land for growing crops or rearing animals (6)

12 These remain after wood or paper have been completely burnt (5)

13 A walkway between seats in a church or cinema (5)

15 These provide light (5)

16 Funny faces made of paper or plastic which we can wear at a party (5)

18 Move a spoon in a cup or bowl to mix the contents (4)

New words I have learned

_____

_____

Name _____

Date _____

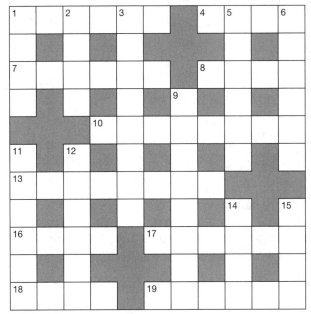

WORD LIST

ABLE	EGGS	SOFT
ARCS	EIGHTY	SPHERE
ASSETS	FOURTH	STABLE
BALLOONS	HOUR	STRAIGHT
BRIDGE	KNEE	TRIANGLE
BUZZ	RING	ZIGZAG
CORNER	ROTATING	

Anagram

Find the word in the crossword that has the anagram ALTERING .

_____

Words from Words

Find five words of four letters or more using the letters of 10-across.

_____

_____

Across

1. A perfectly round, solid figure; a ball (6)
4. I am usually – – – – to finish my homework in two hours (4)
7. The one after the third (6)
8. Jewelry in the shape of a circle (4)
10. A line can also be called a – – – – – – – – angle (8)
13. A figure with three sides and three angles (8)
16. The sound made by bees (4)
17. The place in a room where two walls meet at right angles (6)
18. These are oval in shape (and can be eaten) (4)
19. The money and property that a person or business owns (6)

5. People and vehicles use this to cross over a river or railway (6)
6. Four times twenty (6)
9. Party items that are blown up to form round or long shapes (8)
11. A shelter for horses; firm and not likely to tip over (6)
12. A line which turns up and down, up and down, up and down (6)
14. A joint in the leg (4)
15. Parts of the circumference of a circle (4)

Down

1. The opposite of hard (4)
2. This consists of sixty minutes (4)
3. Going round and round from a fixed point (8)

New words I have learned

_____

_____

_____

Level C **Unit 34**
(Answers on page 60)

Hidden Words

Three words in the crossword are hidden in this sentence.

WE WERE TOLD THAT CHESS CLUBS MEET ON THE SECOND OR SIXTH WEEK OF TERM–OTHER CLUBS DO, TOO.

_____ _____

_____

Across

1. Young birds (6)
3. An insect that flies at night and is attracted to light (4)
7. African antelopes (4)
8. A young swan (6)
10. A big round fish (7)
11. When we burn paper and other garbage, only this remains (3)
12. Short for advertisement (2)
13. Large American vultures (7)
15. Big flightless birds which became extinct a long time ago (6)
17. A wild pig (4)
18. Two or more father sheep (4)
19. A sheep which has not yet been shorn has a – – – – – – back (6)

Down

1. Some people keep birds in these (5)
2. A large lizard (6)
4. If I – – – a pet, I must take good care of it (3)
5. Come out of the egg (5)
6. Large, nonpoisonous snakes (7)
9. Small, colored birds (7)
11. A type of salamander from Mexico with a very strange name (7)
12. A snake whose name suggests that it is good at math (5)
14. Word used for a cat or dog which has no home or owner (5)
16. A barrier to reduce the flow of water; a pond for water on a farm (3)

Anagram

Find the word in the crossword which has the anagram MARS.

_____

New words I have learned

_____

_____

Name _____

Date _____

 **Unit 35**
(Answers on page 60)

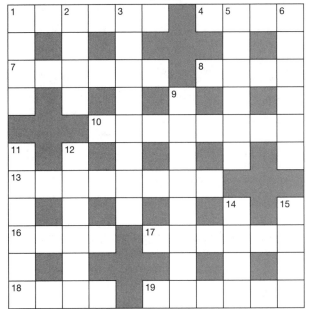

Write the words in the crossword using this different version of a well-known story. If you are not sure which word belongs in a space, leave it and come back to it later.

This is the story of three (1-across) (18-across), two boy (18-across) and a girl named (8-across) who was very clever, but gentle as a (4-across). They were a very happy and (3-down) (2-down). One day, they decided that they shouldn't (15-down) at home any longer and that they were big enough to leave home and build their own houses. They asked their mother and she agreed as long as they promised to visit her every week. She told them, however, about a very nasty (5-down), a (19-across) (14-down) which loved to eat (1-across) (18-across). They promised that they would be careful and immediately set off to build their houses.

The first of the three (1-across) (18-across) saw a nice, big (10-across) in a field, and he went to the farmer and politely (9-down, two words) some of it for his house. Soon his house was complete. The second one found a big pile of (7-across), and he took them away. Soon his house was complete,

and the brothers went to see how their sister, (8-across), was getting on. She had decided to build her house of (6-down). It took much longer to build it, but her brothers helped her. Their arms were (12-down) from all the (17-across) and from carrying all those (6-down), but finally (8-across) had a lovely little house.

The three (1-across) (18-across) knew the (19-across) (14-down) would soon (11-down, two words), and they sat down in their houses to (16-across) for him to come. At (1-down) he came to the house of the first brother. (13-across, two words) out in a loud voice, "I'm going to huff and puff and blow your house down." And, of course, he did! The first brother then ran to the house of the second brother, and so did the (14-down). Very soon the (14-down) had blown down the second house, and the brothers ran to their sister's house and locked the door. The (14-down) tried very hard to blow down the house made of (6-down), but he couldn't, and he went away very angry. As he walked off, the three (1-across) (18-across) shouted after him, "Ha-ha! We tricked you! We always intended to live together in the brick house. We built those two flimsy houses only to annoy you!"

New words I have learned

_____

_____

_____

Name _____

Date _____

Level C Unit 36
(Answers on page 60)

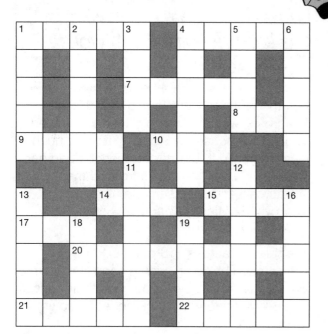

Hidden Message

Take the first letter of every word in the paragraph to read the hidden message.

GREG IS VERY EXCITED. YESTERDAY, OUR UNCLE ROBERT SENT EXTRA LONG FAXES TO WARN OF GHOSTLY, OLD, LIVELY DRAGONS SCHEMING TO ATTACK RIVER STREET! _____

_____

Across

1. After our vacation, we will put some photographs in this (5)
4. Astronauts travel through – – – – – (5)
7. When we go to Hong Kong for a vacation, we will travel in this (9)
8. Everyone and everything (3)
9. When I went to Greece, I was able to – – – – my cousins for the first time (4)
10. To go to another state, we can go by train or car, or we can – – – (3)
14. To go to school, some pupils travel on this (3)
15. Before starting our vacation, we must put our clothes in these (4)
17. Before airplanes existed, people used to travel to Europe by – – – (3)
20. Some very important people have this person to protect them when they travel (9)
21. Everyone – – – – – a vacation from work and school (5)
22. In Captain Cook's time, ships needed these to enable the wind to blow them along (5)

Down

1. I may have to set this to help me to wake up and get ready for my vacation (5)
2. Long, flat-bottomed boats that carry goods on canals and rivers (6)
3. We need these to show us where a street or a town or a country is (4)
4. Small creatures found in the garden which move very, very slowly (6)
5. If I give my telephone number to a friend in another state or country, I must start with the – – – – code (4)
6. When we want to catch a train, it is better to be – – – – – than late (5)
11. When we go on tours to very interesting places, it is helpful to have these people to explain things to us (6)
12. An African word for an adventurous tour or expedition (6)
13. A word to describe people and things from the world's largest continent (5)
16. In every competitive team sport and in every argument, there are at least two of these (5)
18. Everyone should be – – – – to swim (4)
19. Most people of all – – – – like to travel (4)

Level C **Unit 37**

(Answers on page 60)

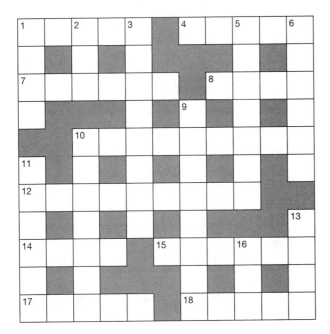

Hidden Words

Find the three words in the crossword that are hidden in this paragraph.

WE WENT TO THE BEACH AND LEFT OUR THINGS ON OUR TOWELS. BUT, LATER, WE COULDN'T FIND OUR LUNCH OR SEASHELLS WE HAD COLLECTED. MAX DID A WAR DANCE AS HE WATCHED A SEAGULL GOBBLE HIS SANDWICHES AND SCATTER HIS SHELLS.

_____ _____

_____

Across

1. A large string instrument much bigger than a violin (5)
4. A prize or certificate for some achievement (5)
7. Bends over, perhaps to pick up something (6)
8. A piece of cloth on the mast of a boat or ship, used to catch the wind (4)
10. The day before today (9)
12. Ten, nine, eight, seven, six, five, four, three, two, one, zero (9)
14. Pieces of old cloth or clothing (4)
15. The part of the tool or knife which we hold (6)
17. A quadruped which people ride (5)
18. A country where archaeologists are at work (5)

Down

1. A container or box in which things can be kept and protected (4)
2. In stories, a name for a lion (3)
3. Situated on the other side; The – – – – – – – – sides of a rectangle are equal (8)
5. When this man rubbed a magic lamp, a genie appeared (7)
6. Postpones; puts off for the time being (6)
9. Add ornaments to make a room (or a birthday cake) look pretty (8)
10. Not as old (7)
11. Burn slightly, for example with an iron (6)
13. Good, better, – – – – (4)
16. The hours between sunrise and sunset (3)

Hidden Message

An unwanted letter appears many times in this sentence. When you have discovered which letter it is, cross it out where it does not belong and read the sentence.

OMOYO DOOGO SOOMEOTOIMOESO OFOIGOHTOS WOITOHO OOURO COAT OANOD WOITHO OTHEOIR DOOOGOSO.

_____

New words I have learned

_____

_____

Level C **Unit 38**
(Answers on page 60)

Fruits and Vegetables

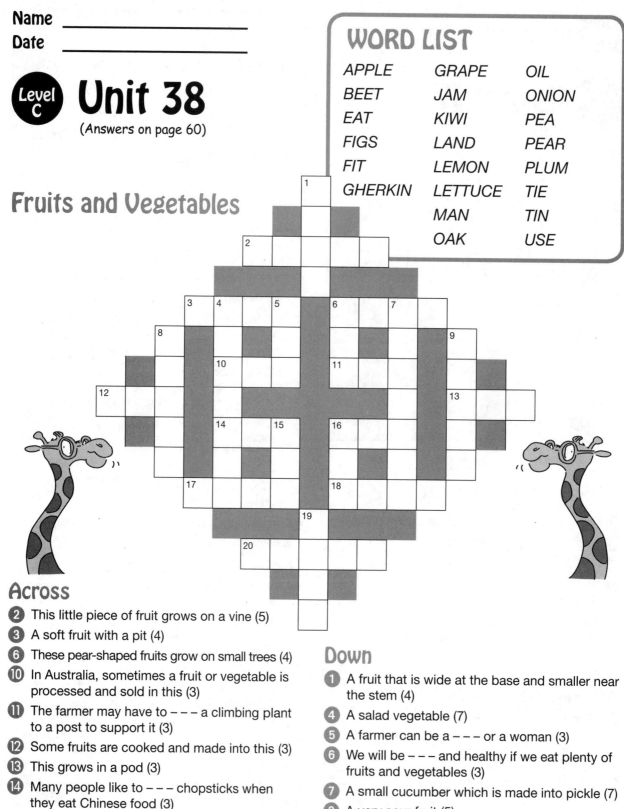

Across

2 This little piece of fruit grows on a vine (5)

3 A soft fruit with a pit (4)

6 These pear-shaped fruits grow on small trees (4)

10 In Australia, sometimes a fruit or vegetable is processed and sold in this (3)

11 The farmer may have to – – – a climbing plant to a post to support it (3)

12 Some fruits are cooked and made into this (3)

13 This grows in a pod (3)

14 Many people like to – – – chopsticks when they eat Chinese food (3)

16 Some animals like to eat acorns from this tree (3)

17 – – – – root is a dark red vegetable which we may eat in a salad (4)

18 Farmers grow their crops on this (4)

20 A vegetable that may bring tears to your eyes if you cut it when it is raw (5)

Down

1 A fruit that is wide at the base and smaller near the stem (4)

4 A salad vegetable (7)

5 A farmer can be a – – – or a woman (3)

6 We will be – – – and healthy if we eat plenty of fruits and vegetables (3)

7 A small cucumber which is made into pickle (7)

8 A very sour fruit (5)

9 A very popular fruit (5)

15 Put food into the mouth, chew, and swallow (3)

16 We may use this when we fry food (3)

19 A small fuzzy, brown-skinned fruit with green flesh on the inside (4)

Food Rhymes

What can we eat or drink that rhymes with the words below?

(A) CHAPEL _____

(B) DAUGHTER _____

(C) FED _____

(D) FREEZE _____

(E) FUNNY _____

(F) PARROTS _____

(G) SCENES _____

(H) SHAPES _____

(I) SHIPS _____

(J) SHUTTER _____

(K) SILK _____

(L) TICKLES _____

(M) WE _____

(N) WISH _____

Question and Answer

In this sentence, some of the words are written correctly, but not all. When you have discovered how to read the question, rewrite it correctly and then give your answer.

NI MY REWARD I EVAH TEN EULB SOCKS DNA TEN DER SOCKS. HTIW MY SEYE CLOSED, WOH MANY SKCOS MUST I TAKE MORF MY REWARD IF I WANT OT BE ERUS OF GNITTEG A RIAP OF EHT SAME ROLOC ?

_____

_____

_____

_____ Answer: _____

Words from Words

Make four words of <u>three letters or more</u> using the letters of 7-down in the crossword.

_____ _____

_____ _____

_____

New words I have learned

_____

_____

_____

Level C Unit 39
(Answers on page 60)

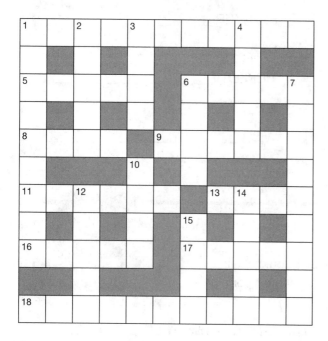

WORD LIST

ALIGN	OVALS
AMIGO	PAIL
BATH	PALE
EASTER	PEACE
ELEPHANTS	PIECE
KNEAD	ROSE
LIES	SALES
MIDDLE	SHOULDERS
MISCHIEVOUS	SOLID
NEED	SUPERMARKET

Across

1 A large store where food and other goods are sold (11)

5 Egg-shaped figures (5)

6 A part or a bit of something (5)

8 My cat always – – – – in a sunny place in winter (4)

9 The center (6)

11 An annual Christian holiday (6)

13 A place where we can wash ourselves (4)

16 A prism is the name given to some – – – – – shapes (5)

17 When we match things up in a line, we say we – – – – – them (5)

18 Playfully naughty (11)

Down

1 The parts of the body to which the upper arms are attached (9)

2 Absence of conflict (5)

3 Got up or stood up (4)

4 Press and stretch dough for bread making (5)

6 Another name for a bucket (4)

7 Large animals with trunks (9)

10 Require (4)

12 Stores have these to dispose of goods at reduced prices (5)

14 A Spanish word for friend (5)

15 Having very little color (4)

New words I have learned

_____

_____

_____

You Write the Clues

¹B	O	O	²K	S		³B	⁴T
E			H			A	E
⁵E	N	⁶D		⁷O	R	G	A N

(crossword grid showing letters: BOOKS, BIT, HAE, ORGAN, END, DOO, POP, MUGS, CARS, MAI, RADIO, RED, CAT, HID, HORSE)

Homophones and Homonyms

A Homophones are words which have the same sound but different spelling and different meanings. Find the three pairs of homophones in the Word List (page 44).

_____ and _____ ,

_____ and _____ ,

_____ and _____

B Homonyms are words which have the same spelling but different meanings. There are two four-letter words in the Word List each of which has two different meanings.

_____ _____

Write your own clues for the crossword above, first the across clues and then the down clues. You may like to get help from a dictionary. Compare your clues with those your friends have written.

Across

1 _____

3 _____

5 _____

7 _____

8 _____

9 _____

12 _____

14 _____

16 _____

17 _____

Down

1 _____

2 _____

3 _____

4 _____

6 _____

8 _____

10 _____

11 _____

13 _____

15 _____

Level C · Unit 40

(Answers on page 60)

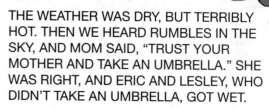

Hidden Words

Find four words from the crossword that are hidden in the following paragraph.

THE WEATHER WAS DRY, BUT TERRIBLY HOT. THEN WE HEARD RUMBLES IN THE SKY, AND MOM SAID, "TRUST YOUR MOTHER AND TAKE AN UMBRELLA." SHE WAS RIGHT, AND ERIC AND LESLEY, WHO DIDN'T TAKE AN UMBRELLA, GOT WET.

_____ _____

_____ _____

Across

1 The land near the sea (5)

4 We put this on an envelope before we mail the letter (5)

7 A street which often has trees on either side (6)

8 An image that is worshipped as a god; a word in the TV show, "American – – – –" (4)

10 The people in a store who are buying things (9)

12 The best known Australian animals (9)

14 Use speech; discuss (4)

15 We may put this on our bread (6)

17 This is how some metals become if exposed to moisture (5)

18 A very large number of flying insects such as bees (5)

Down

1 Use your hands to show that you enjoyed the concert (4)

2 A tool used to chop wood (3)

3 The day before Friday (8)

5 The number of the house and the street and city in which you live (7)

6 Shine; from Poland (6)

9 The large, brown, hard fruit of a palm tree which contain a milky liquid (8)

10 We can light these when the electricity goes out (7)

11 Someone who moves on the ice or other surfaces wearing special boots (6)

13 An instrument in a band or orchestra that is played with sticks (4)

16 A hot drink (3)

New words I have learned

_____

_____

_____

Level C **Unit 41**
(Answers on page 61)

WORD LIST

ABOLISHED	OCEAN	SCHOOL
AVOID	OMIT	SEVEN
EAGLE	ORCHESTRA	SHARE
END	PEACH	STOP
HER	PIANO	TITLE
HERO	PLAIN	VIDEO
HIDE	POLO	WEEK
NEEDS	RESCUE	WRONG

Words from Words

Make four words of <u>four letters or more</u> using letters from 19-across in the crossword.

_____ _____

_____ _____

Anagram

Find the word in the Word List which has the anagram HAS BOILED.

_____

Across

1. A musical instrument with a keyboard (5)
4. The number of days in the week (5)
7. Got rid of, or put an end to, a rule or practice (9)
8. The opposite of begin (3)
9. Go to a place where you cannot be found (4)
10. A ball game played on horseback (4)
13. A period of seven days (4)
14. Don't continue (4)
17. Belonging to a woman or girl; she did – – – homework (3)
19. A large group of musicians (9)
20. A very big bird of prey (5)
21. A very large sea (5)

6. Requires (5)
11. Save someone from danger or from another bad situation (6)
12. Enjoy together (5)
13. The opposite of right (5)
15. Name of a book (5)
16. Simple; without decoration (5)
18. Someone whom people admire; a person who does very good or brave acts (4)

Down

1. A yellowish soft fruit with a pit (5)
2. Keep away from (5)
3. Leave out; don't put in (4)
4. The place where we learn (6)
5. We sometimes borrow this so that we can watch a movie (5)

New words I have learned

_____

_____

_____

Level C **Unit 42**

(Answers on page 61)

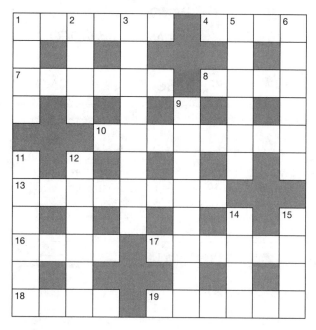

Across

1. Wildlife is found in this wooded area (6)
4. An animal which sleeps through much of the winter (4)
7. Any living thing that is not a plant (6)
8. The soft feathers of young birds (4)
10. A slow-moving animal which has a shell (8)
13. Some big companies act as – – – – – – – – for wildlife protection (8)
16. A small amphibian with strong back legs for leaping (4)
17. An insect which makes a shrill sound in summer (6)
18. We put a name on a dog's collar, so it won't be – – – – (4)
19. Hard covers which protect clams and oysters (6)

Down

1. A very young horse (4)
2. All people and animals depend on this water from the clouds (4)
3. A small fish that looks rather like a horse (8)

WORD LIST

ANIMAL   FOAL   SHELLS
BATS   FOREST   SPONSORS
BEAR   FROG   STARFISH
CICADA   LOST   TALL
DODOES   RAIN   TORTOISE
DOWN   RANGER   USEFUL
EXOTIC   SEAHORSE

Anagram

Find the word in the crossword that has the anagram HE'S A ROSE.

_____

Words from Words

Find five words of <u>four letters or more</u> using the letters of 10-across.

_____   _____

_____   _____

_____

5. A word used to describe animals and plants that are not native to our country (6)
6. An official who patrols forests and parks (6)
9. A fish shaped rather like a star (8)
11. Some animals in the world are – – – – – – to us because they pull heavy loads or give us wool (6)
12. Flightless birds that are now extinct (6)
14. A giraffe is a – – – – animal (4)
15. Animals that hang upside down when they sleep (4)

New words I have learned

_____

_____

_____

Name _____

Date _____

 Level C **Unit 43**

(Answers on page 61)

(Answers on page 61)

WORD LIST

BABBLER	FLAT	TEA
BED	HOSED	TOWROPE
CANALS	ICE	VIADUCT
CAPTAIN	ITCH	WADED
DEEP	MIRROR	WATER
DIVERS	OPAL	WET
DRIPPY	POUR OUT	
DROOP	RAINBOW	

Hidden Word

Take a letter from each word in the sentence to find the hidden word. You must discover whether to choose the first, second, third or fourth letter of the words. Guess and check. (The hidden word is <u>not</u> on the Word List.)

BURIED TREASURE RECOVERED– ANTIQUE PLATES, ORNAMENTS, INGOTS, VALUABLE PIECES.

_____

Across

1. People who go down below the water for fun or to work (6)
3. At the beach, sandfly bites may make us – – – – (4)
7. The color of this precious gem is sometimes like blue or green water (4)
8. Waterways made by people to let ships and boats pass through (6)
10. From the jug, I – – – –   – – – drinks for everyone (4, 3)
11. The very bottom of the sea is called the sea – – – (3)
12. When caught in the rain, we get – – – (3)
13. After rain we may see this in the sky (7)
15. A very – – – – – – faucet wastes water; we should turn the faucet off properly (6)
17. When a fizzy drink has lost all its bubbles, we say it has become – – – – (4)
18. We must be good swimmers before we go into water of this kind (4)
19. When we can see our reflection in a pool, we say it is like a – – – – – – (6)

Down

1. When there is not enough rain, the flowers – – – – – (5)
2. A bridge for carrying a road or railway over a deep valley (7)
4. A drink made with boiling water (3)
5. Used garden equipment to water the garden (5)
6. The person in command of a ship (7)
9. A big boat may use this to pull along a smaller boat (7)
11. One who talks excessively (7)
12. Walked through deep water (5)
14. The main subject of this crossword (5)
16. Frozen water (3)

New words I have learned

_____

_____

Name _____

Date _____

(Answers on page 61)

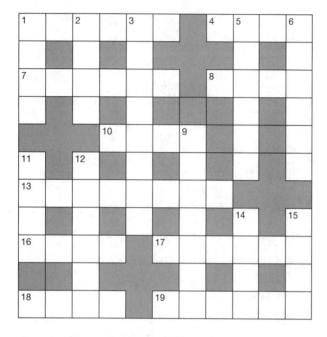

Hidden Words

Two words from the crossword are hiding in this sentence.

WHY IS JAKE'S CAP EXTREMELY WET?
SOME KID LEFT IT IN THE RAIN.

_____ _____

Across

1. One that searches for something, such as animals (6)
4. A type of fish; of low pitch (4)
7. A figure with four equal sides and four right angles (6)
8. This is what we eat (4)
10. To make cloudy or confuse (4)
13. This protects us from the rain (8)
16. A violent disturbance of the peace by a crowd of people (4)
17. Money paid back for returned goods (6)
18. A form of physical and mental exercise and relaxation of Hindu origin (4)
19. Run away from control or danger; some prisoners try to – – – – – – from prison (6)

Down

1. We use this to water the garden (4)
2. In grammar, a naming word (4)
3. Put on a register as a member of a group, school, etc. (8)
5. On every side; an island has water all – – – – – – it (6)
6. The capital city of New South Wales (6)
9. Revolving cylinders which is used to press, shape, spread, or smooth something (7)
11. A low sound that a contented or pleased cat makes (4)
12. Another word for rectangle (6)
14. A type of fish which we may buy in a can (4)
15. Having nothing to do (4)

New words I have learned

_____

_____

Name _____

Date _____

 Level C **Unit 45**

(Answers on page 61)

(Answers on page 61)

WORD LIST

ATE	HOPS	SCENTS
BEDS	LAUGH	SENSE
CIRCLE	LIP	STEAL
DANCE	LORD	STEEL
DECIDE	ONE	STRAW
EAST	RECORDERS	TUG
ESCAPE	ROWED	VICTORIAN
EVEN	SCENE	WIPE

Words Inside Words

Some words in the crossword have other words inside them. Write these words from the Word List, underlining the words inside them which mean:

A Something which is one-hundredth of a dollar _____

B Person who is the winner in a contest

_____

C To be in debt to someone

_____

D Something to wear on the head

_____

E String made from twisted strands

_____

F Not cooked _____

Across

1 Take something without permission and without intending to return it (5)

4 A hard metal; some saucepans are made of stainless – – – – – (5)

7 Small wooden musical instruments played by blowing air into them (9)

8 Pull hard or suddenly (3)

9 Use a cloth to dry or clean something (4)

10 Had something to eat (3)

14 A part of the mouth (3)

15 We sleep in these at night (4)

17 The first counting number (3)

20 Anything related to the reign of Queen Victoria of England (9)

21 Move the body in time with the music (5)

22 Landscape; in a story, the place where something happens (5)

Down

1 Dried stalks of grain; something we may use to drink a milkshake (5)

2 Break free from, and run away from something that is holding us (6)

3 The title of a book with three parts written by J.R.R. Tolkien is "The – – – – of the Rings" (4)

4 Perfumes; smells (6)

5 The opposite of west (4)

6 We do this when we hear a really funny joke (5)

11 A perfectly round shape (6)

12 Make up your mind (6)

13 Used the oars in a boat on the water (5)

16 Sometimes people say, "Use your common – – – – –" (5)

18 A number is either odd or – – – – (4)

19 Moves by jumping on one foot (4)

Name _____

Date _____

Level C Unit 46
(Answers on page 61)

WORD LIST

ANTS	NAVIGATE	SCENERY
ARSON	OASIS	SEE
ASLEEP	OTTERS	SIGHTSEER
ATLANTIC	PINES	SUNBURN
CALLS	REEF	TWELVE
EEL	SAFARI	USES
EMUS	SANCTUARY	

Hidden Message

An unwanted letter appears many times in this sentence. When you have discovered which letter it is, cross it out and read the sentence.

SIFS SYOUS SGOS SONS SANS SEXCURSIONS SINS STHES SWILDS, SCOUNTS SHOWS SMANYS SBIRDS SCALLSS SYOUS SCANS SHEARS.

Across

1 The crime of setting fire to houses and other buildings (5)

4 A green and fertile spot in a desert (5)

7 The number of months in a year (6)

8 A ridge of jagged rock, coral, or sand; The Great Barrier – – – – (4)

10 A person who goes round looking at interesting things and places (9)

12 A place of refuge and safety for wildlife (9)

14 Large birds which do not fly (4)

15 Fish-eating mammals with long bodies, fur, and webbed feet (6)

17 Trees with needle-shaped leaves (5)

18 Cries out to attract someone's attention (5)

6 An expedition to see wild animals in their natural habitat (6)

9 One of the five great oceans of the world (8)

10 We get this when we forget to put on a sunscreen (7)

11 Not awake (6)

13 The teacher – – – – a compass to show us where the North is (4)

16 A long fish which looks rather like a snake (3)

Down

1 Small busy insects (4)

2 Notice; observe (3)

3 Direct the course of a ship, aircraft, or vehicle (8)

5 The natural landscape which we see around us (7)

New words I have learned

_____

_____

_____

_____

Level C **Unit 47**
(Answers on page 61)

Three Blind Mice

Write the words in the crossword using this different version of Three Blind Mice. If you are not sure which word belongs in a space, leave it and come back to it later.

In the Word List there are three words which must have apostrophes. But in crossword grids, words are always written without punctuation.

On a – – – – (1-down) with lots of cows, goats, and ducks lives a – – – – – – – (7-down) – – – – (6-across). One day she hears a funny noise. "What is it? Is it – – – (11-across) – – – (10-across)?" she asks, "or can it be a – – – (5-down)?"

"– – – (6-down) are you?" she calls. Then she sees a little twitching nose and she shouts, "– – – (14-across) those naughty – – – – – (2-across) – – – – – (20-across) – – – – (19-down)!" She starts to – – – (12-across) and the – – – – (19-down) – – – (12-across) after her.

But then she remembers – – – (16-across) carving – – – – – (9-down). Quickly she – – – – – (8-down) it. "– – – (13-across) get those naughty – – – –

(19-down)," she cries as she waves the – – – – – (9-down) in the air. She isn't – – – – (17-across) to catching – – – – (19-down), but she is lucky and it turns out to be quite – – – – (18-across). With one sweep of her – – – – – (9-down), she cuts off all three tails.

The poor tailless – – – – – – – (4-down) – – – (12-across) away as fast as they can, feeling very – – – (15-down), and hoping that their tails will grow again. And – – – (16-across) – – – – – – – (7-down) – – – – (6-across) says to herself, "If I see those – – – – (19-down) – – – – (3-across) again, – – – (13-across) – – – (16-down) knots in their whiskers!"

(Word List is located on page 54.)

WORD LIST

BLIND	IT'S (it is)	THREE
CAT	KNIFE	TIE
EASY	MICE	USED
EVER	OUR	VICTIMS
FARM	RAT	WHO
FARMER'S	RUN	WIFE
FINDS	SAD	
I'LL (I will)	THE	

Words from Words

Make five words of three letters or more using the letters of 7-down in the crossword.

_____ _____

_____ _____

_____

The Revenge of the Mice!

Write a short story telling how the three mice get their revenge. Remember that they are blind!

_____

_____

_____

_____

_____

_____

_____

_____

Hidden Information

In this sentence, every other word is written incorrectly; when you have discovered how to read these words, you will be able to read the sentence.

ON SRAM THERE ERA ABOUT ECIWT AS YNAM DAYS NI A RAEY AS EREHT ARE NO EARTH. FI YOU ERA NINE SRAEY OLD WON, YOU DLUOW BE YLNO FOUR-DNA-A-FLAH ON SRAM.

_____

_____

_____

_____

 Level C

Unit 48
(Answers on page 61)

WORD LIST

ABLE	LESSON
BEACH	OPEN
CITIZENSHIP	PEARS
DEEP	PRICE
DIVER	PRINT
ELVES	REEF
ENVIRONMENT	RUNNERS-UP
EXPERT	SPICE
EXPLORERS	SPIN
FREE	VOICE

Across

1. Everything which surrounds us, in nature or made by people (11)
5. The cost of an item (5)
6. A person who goes down under the water for sport or to work (5)
8. The opposite of shut (4)
9. Something that we learn (6)
11. A person who knows a lot about a particular subject or skill (6)
13. Are cats really – – – – to see in the dark? (4)
16. Something which is used to flavor sweet or savory food, e.g., cinnamon (5)
17. Fruit which are wide at one end and narrow near the stalk (5)
18. A person who comes from another country and would like to become American can apply for this (11)

Down

1. Brave people, such as Lewis and Clark, who traveled to unknown parts of America (9)
2. I use this when I speak, shout, or sing (5)
3. A ridge of rocks or coral just below the surface of the sea (4)
4. In fairy tales, little people with pointed ears (5)
6. Goes down a long way; the water in one end of the pool is very – – – – (4)
7. The ones who come second in a competition (7-2)
10. Not tied up; able to go anywhere (4)
12. Write words without joining the letters together (5)
14. The sandy shore by the sea (5)
15. Turn round and round in a circle very quickly; use machinery to turn wool or cotton into thread (4)

New words I have learned

_____

_____

_____

Hidden Words

Three words from the crossword are hidden in the following sentence:

I TOLD DAD I VERY MUCH WANT TO BE A CHAMPION SWIMMER, BUT HE SAID THAT IT INVOLVES A LOT OF PRESSURE, EFFORT, AND DAILY PRACTICE.

_____ _____ _____

Level A - Answers

Unit 1   Page 5

Anagram
15-across, SENT

Unit 2   Page 6

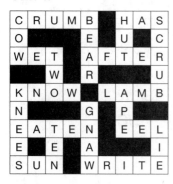

Silent Letters
1-across, CRUMB;
11-down, GNAW;
8-down, KNEES;
8-across KNOW;
9-across, LAMB;
17-across, WRITE

Hidden Word
2-down, BEAR
(TO <u>BE A R</u>ADIO HOST)

Unit 3   Page 7

Unit 4   Page 8

Words in Words
5-across, CENT;
14-across, RAID; 6-
across, OAT; 11-across,
ONE; 11-down, ORE;
9-down, EAT; 13-down, IN;
12-across, IT

Hidden Words
The third letter of each
word, GOOD WORK

Unit 5   Page 9

Anagram
6-down, DOORS

Hidden Words
16-across, MAT;
15-across, SOW
(MET SA<u>M AT</u> THE
SHOPS <u>SO WE</u>)

Unit 6   Page 10

Hidden Word
12-across, POST

Which Word?
7-across, NEWS

Unit 7   Page 11

Anagram
4-down, STEAMSHIP

Unit 8   Page 12

Anagram
7-down, EARTH

Words from Words
VIOLET: let, lie, lit, live, lot,
love, oil, olive, tie, tile, toe,
toil, veil, veto, vote, *and
more*

Level A – Answers

Unit 9   Page 13

Anagrams
5-down, SLOW;
17-across, EAR;
13-down, EAST

Word Pairs
FISH SHOP, HUGE
FISH, HUGE PAGE,
HUGE TOWN, HUGE
TENT, SLOW RUN,
STARFISH, WET
WOOD, WOOD SHOP
and others

Unit 10   Page 14

Hidden Word
8-across, PONY (I put
your book up on your
locker)

Anagram
8-down, PEACH

Unit 11   Page 15

Unit 12   Page 16

Which Word?
SENDS; ENDS

Anagram
5-across, SILVER

Unit 13   Page 17

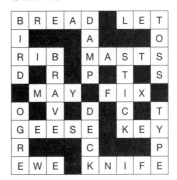

Anagram
6-down, BRAVE

Hidden Words
EWE, STICK
(AT HOME WE FLY
OUR PLASTIC KITE)

Unit 14   Page 18

Hidden Word
7-across, TRIO

Anagram
18-across, LEMONADE

Unit 15   Page 19

Unit 16   Page 20

Which Word?
Ⓐ BRIGHT, RIGHT
Ⓑ USE, US

Level B – Answers

Unit 17   Page 21

Words in Words
7-across, GONE; 9-across, NOTE; 2-down, NUGGET; 1-across, SCENT; 10-down, TABLE; 11-across, USER

Hidden Message
ANYONE WHO CAN READ THIS MESSAGE IS VERY CLEVER

Unit 18   Page 22

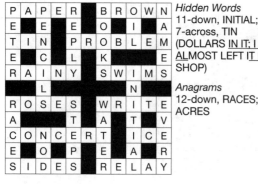

Hidden Words
11-down, INITIAL; 7-across, TIN (DOLLARS IN IT; I ALMOST LEFT IT IN THE SHOP)

Anagrams
12-down, RACES; CARES, ACRES

Unit 19   Page 23

Unit 20   Page 24

Unit 21   Page 25

Words from Words
13-across, TAILORS: air, also, art, last, list, lost, lot, oar, oil, rat, roast, sail, salt, sat, sit, soil, stair, star, *and more*

Unit 22   Page 26

Anagram
11-down, ALLOWED

Words in Words
A 4-across, HABIT (bit); **B** 16-across, CHEAPER (heap); **C** 1-across, LINKS (ink); **D** 14-across, SPLIT (lit); **E** 11-down, ALLOWED (low); **F** 10-across, DRAKE (rake); **G** 14-down, SCRUB (rub); **H** 2-down, NOTHING (thin)

Unit 23   Page 27

Hidden Words
17-across, HOP (IN THE SHOP); 9-across, REAL (WERE ALL FROM); 13-down, WHOLE (THOSE WHO LEFT); 3-down, HEEL (THE ELEVATOR)

Unit 24   Page 28

Anagram
3-Down, WIDER

Backward Words
A 5-down, NUMERALS (are); **B** 6-across, DEBT (bed); **C** 13-across, AREA (era); **D** 9-across, TILE (lit); **E** 10-down, LINES (nil); **F** 3-down, WIDER (red); **G** 7-across, RISE (sir)

Level B & C – Answers

Unit 25 — Page 29

Anagram
16-across, NOTHING

Hidden Word
4-down, LEARN

Unit 29 — Page 33

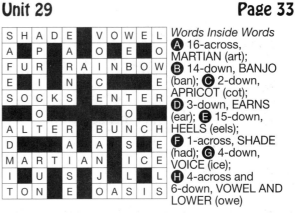

Words Inside Words
A 16-across, MARTIAN (art);
B 14-down, BANJO (ban);
C 2-down, APRICOT (cot);
D 3-down, EARNS (ear);
E 15-down, HEELS (eels);
F 1-across, SHADE (had);
G 4-down, VOICE (ice);
H 4-across and 6-down, VOWEL AND LOWER (owe)

Unit 26 — Page 30

Unit 30 — Page 34

Hidden Words
19-down, SNOW (TENNIS NO WONDER);
8-across, RAM (READY FOR A MILKSHAKE)

Unit 27 — Page 31

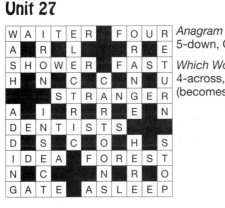

Anagram
5-down, ORANGE

Which Word?
4-across, FOUR (becomes OUR)

Unit 31 — Page 35

Anagram
10-down, TUESDAY

Hidden Word
BEETLE

Unit 28 — Page 32

Hidden Word
14-down, REELS

Unit 32 — Page 36

Words from Words
SPACESHIP: aces, ache, ashes, caps, case, cash, chase, chess, heaps, hips, pace, pass, peas, pies, pipe, seas, shape, sips, spice, spies, *and more*

Anagram
19-across, SOMETIMES

Level C – Answers

Unit 33　　　　Page 37

Anagram
13-across, TRIANGLE

Words from Words
STRAIGHT: artist, hair, hats, hits, rats, right, shirt, sight, stair, star, start, stir, tart, that, this, tight, *and more*

Unit 34　　　　Page 38

Anagram
18-across, RAMS

Hidden Words
5-down, HATCH
(THAT CHESS CLUBS);
13-across, CONDORS
(THE SECOND OR SIXTH);
3-across, MOTH
(OF TERM – OTHER)

Unit 35　　　　Page 39

Unit 36　　　　Page 40

Hidden Message
GIVE YOURSELF TWO GOLD STARS.

Unit 37　　　　Page 41

Hidden Message
MY DOG SOMETIMES FIGHTS WITH OUR CAT AND WITH THEIR DOGS.

Hidden Words
15-across, HANDLE
(BEACH AND LEFT);
17-across, HORSE
(LUNCH OR SEASHELLS);
4-across, AWARD
(DID A WAR DANCE)

Unit 38　　　　Pages 42–43

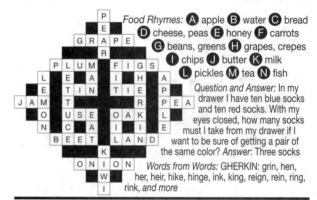

Food Rhymes: Ⓐ apple Ⓑ water Ⓒ bread Ⓓ cheese, peas Ⓔ honey Ⓕ carrots Ⓖ beans, greens Ⓗ grapes, crepes Ⓘ chips Ⓙ butter Ⓚ milk Ⓛ pickles Ⓜ tea Ⓝ fish

Question and Answer: In my drawer I have ten blue socks and ten red socks. With my eyes closed, how many socks must I take from my drawer if I want to be sure of getting a pair of the same color? *Answer:* Three socks

Words from Words: GHERKIN: grin, hen, her, heir, hike, hinge, ink, king, reign, rein, ring, rink, *and more*

Unit 39　　　　Pages 44–45

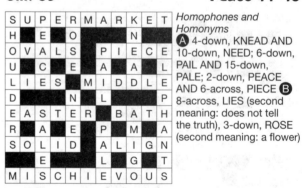

Homophones and Homonyms
Ⓐ 4-down, KNEAD AND 10-down, NEED; 6-down, PAIL AND 15-down, PALE; 2-down, PEACE AND 6-across, PIECE Ⓑ
8-across, LIES (second meaning: does not tell the truth), 3-down, ROSE (second meaning: a flower)

Unit 40　　　　Page 46

Hidden Words
15-across, BUTTER
(BUT TERRIBLY);
13-down, DRUM
(HEARD RUMBLES);
17-across, RUSTY
(TRUST YOUR);
10-down, CANDLES
(ERIC AND LESLEY)

Level C – Answers

Unit 41   Page 47

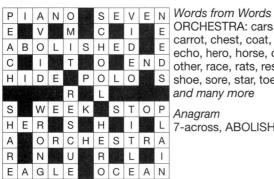

Words from Words
ORCHESTRA: cars, carrot, chest, coat, echo, hero, horse, oars, other, race, rats, rest, shoe, sore, star, toes, *and many more*

Anagram
7-across, ABOLISHED

Unit 42   Page 48

Anagram
3-down, SEAHORSE

Words from Words
TORTOISE: otter, rest, rise, root, rose, sore, sort, store, test, toes, tore, tries, trot, *and more*

Unit 43   Page 49

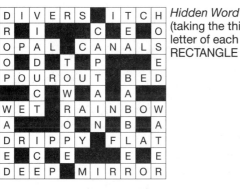

Hidden Word
(taking the third letter of each word)
RECTANGLE

Unit 44   Page 50

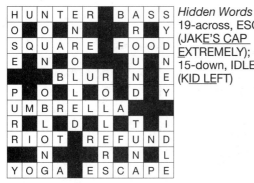

Hidden Words
19-across, ESCAPE
(JAKE'S CAP EXTREMELY);
15-down, IDLE
(KID LEFT)

Unit 45   Page 51

Words Inside Words
Ⓐ SCENTS;
Ⓑ VICTORIAN;
Ⓒ ROWED;
Ⓓ ESCAPE;
Ⓔ RECORDERS;
Ⓕ STRAW

Unit 46   Page 52

Hidden Message
IF YOU GO ON AN EXCURSION IN THE WILD, COUNT HOW MANY BIRD CALLS YOU CAN HEAR.

Unit 47   Pages 53–54

Words from Words
FARMER'S: are, arm, ears, far, farm, frame, fear, mare, Mars, ram, safe, sea, *and many more*

Hidden Information
ON MARS THERE ARE ABOUT TWICE AS MANY DAYS IN A YEAR AS THERE ARE ON EARTH. IF YOU ARE NINE YEARS OLD NOW, YOU WOULD BE ONLY FOUR-AND-A-HALF ON MARS.

Unit 48   Page 55

Hidden Words
6-across, DIVER
(DAD I VERY MUCH);
14-down, BEACH
(TO BE A CHAMPION);
3-down, REEF
(PRESSURE, EFFORT)

Word List

A

able
abolished
about
accent
accept
accidents
ache
aching
acorn
actor
ad
adder
adding
addition
address
adds
admit
afraid
after
age
aged
ages
ago
aisle
ajar
Aladdin
alarm
album
align
all
allowed
also
alter
ambulance
amigo
anchor
and
angle
animal
answer
answers
ant

ants
ape
apple
apricot
apricots
arcs
area
arms
around
arrows
arson
art
artist
ash
ashes
Asia
Asian
asked for
asks
asleep
assets
astonish
ate
Atlantic
atlas
atom
aunt
avenue
avoid
awake
award
away
axe
axolotl

B

babbler
babies
bad
badge
bags
bald
balloons
bananas

banjo
banks
bar
barges
bass
bat
bath
bats
beach
beads
beak
bear
bed
beds
bees
beet
began
behind
best
bird
blind
blur
boar
boat
bodyguard
books
brave
bread
bricks
bridge
bright
brown
bud
bump
bunch
bus
buses
butter
buzz

C

cages
calls
canals

candles
canvas
captain
cartoons
case
cash
cat
cave
cello
Celsius
chasing
cheaper
chemist
chicks
cicada
circle
citizenship
clap
cliff
clock
clowns
clue
coast
cobra
coconut
coconuts
coin
come
concert
condors
cone
continued
cooked
core
corner
corrects
cost
countdown
cow
crabs
crafty
crawl
crumb

cub
cube
cubs
cup
customers
cygnet

D

dam
damp
dance
dangerous
dash
day
debt
decide
deck
decorate
deep
deer
delays
den
dentists
dew
did
diet
dinner
dirty
diver
divers
doctor
doctors
dodoes
doe
doors
down
drake
drippy
drips
droop
drops
drum
dull

E

eager
eagle
ear
early
earns
Earth
east
Easter
easy
eat
eaten
echo
edge
editor
editors
eel
effort
egg
eggs
Egypt
eighty
elastic
electric
elephants
elf
elves
empty
emus
end
ends
enrolled
enter
enters
envelope
environment
envy
erased
error
escape
eve
even
evening

ever
every
evil
ewe
ewes
exit
exotic
expenses
expert
explorers

F

fail
fan
farm
farmer
farmer's
fast
feathers
few
fib
figs
film
finches
finds
fins
fish
fist
fit
fix
flap
flat
florist
flour
fly
foal
fog
food
forest
four
fourth
free
frog
fun
fur

Word List

G

gab
gas
gate
geese
gem
gherkin
given
glad
gnaw
gnus
go
goat
gobble
goggles
gone
good
grab
grape
gravy
great
greedy
grow
guests
guides

H

habit
had
handle
happy
has
hat
hatch
hay
haystack
he called
heavy
heel
heels
her
here
hero

hide
hilt
hop
hoped
hops
horse
hose
hosed
hot
hour
hover
huge
humps
hunter
hut

I

I'll (I will)
ice
idea
idle
idol
iguana
imitate
India
initial
insect
into
iron
isle
it's (it is)
itch

J

jam
jester
jockey
judge

K

kangaroos
kennels
key
kitten
kiwi

knead
knee
knees
knife
knot
knots
know
koala

L

laces
lake
lamb
lamps
land
lap
last
lasts
laugh
leap
learn
least
lemon
lemonade
lemons
Leo
less
lesson
let
letter
lettuce
lid
lie
lies
likeable
linen
lines
links
lip
list
little
lizard
locks
log

loose
Lord
lose
loses
lost
love
low
lower
lung

M

man
maps
March
Martian
masks
mason
masts
mat
mate
May
medal
meet
mended
mew
mice
middle
milk
mill
Mimi
mine
minute
mirror
mischievous
miser
money
mosquitos
moth

N

nail
names
nap
navigate

near
need
needle
needs
net
new
news
nod
noise
nose
not
note
notes
nothing
noun
November
nugget
number
numerals
nut

O

oak
oars
oasis
obey
oblong
ocean
off
ogre
oil
omit
once
one
onion
onions
opal
opals
open
opposite
or
orange
orchestra
order

otters
our
oval
ovals
oven
ovens
over
owe
own

P

pad
page
pail
pal
pale
panda
panic
paper
parents
Paris
passed
past
pea
peace
peach
pear
pears
peel
pencil
pencils
pepper
pest
pet
Peter
phones
piano
piece
piglet
pigs
pilot
pin
pineapple
pines

pit
plain
plan
plane
play
plum
poet
polish
polo
polygon
pony
post
pour out
price
print
problem
purr
pyramid
pythons

Q

questions

R

races
radio
rags
rain
rainbow
rainy
raise
ram
rams
ranger
rapid
rat
reach
real
reasons
recorders
rectangle
red
reef
reels
refund

Word List

relay
repeat
reply
rescue
return
rib
right
rigid
ring
riot
rip
rise
rises
roasted
robber
robot
rollers
roof
rope
rose
roses
rotating
row
rowed
rule
run
runners-up
rush
rusty

S

sack
sad
safari
safes
sail
sails
sales
salt
sanctuary
sand
sat
sauce
saucer

says
scarce
scene
scenery
scent
scents
school
scorch
scrub
sea
seahorse
seal
see
seed
seesaw
sends
sense
sent
September
set
seven
shade
share
shed
shell
shells
shin
shiny
shop
short
shoulders
show up
shower
sides
sightseer
sign
signal
silver
sing
sister
six
skater
ski

slam
sleepy
slow
snails
snow
so
socks
soft
solid
sometimes
song
SOS
sow
space
spaceship
spade
spear
sphere
spice
spiders
spin
splinter
split
sponsors
spot
square
stable
stale
stamp
star
starfish
stay
steal
steals
steamship
steel
stem
steps
stick
sticks
stir
stoops
stop

straight
stranger
straw
stray
stump
suddenly
sugar
sun
sunburn
sunfish
supermarket
supports
swamp
swarm
swim
swims
Syndey

T

table
tacks
tadpole
tailors
talk
tall
tap
tape
tasks
taste
tattoo
tea
tear
telephone
ten
tent
term
test
the
thousands
three
throat
thumb
Thursday
ticket

tie
tiger
tile
time
times
timid
tin
tired
title
toe
told
ton
tonsils
too
tool
top
tortoise
toss
total
town
towrope
traded
train
tray
trees
tres
triangle
triangles
trim
trio
true
try
Tuesday
tug
tugs
tuna
tunnel
twelve
twins
two
type

U

umbrella

umpires
unites
up
use
used
useful
user
uses

V

vase
viaduct
victims
Victorian
video
violet
violin
vixen
voice
vowel

W

waded
wafer
wait
waiter
was
wash
water
web
weed
week
weight
were
wet
who
whole
wider
wife
win
wing
wings
wipe
wolf

wood
woolly
wrap
write
writer
wrong

Y

yawn
yesterday
yoga
yolk
younger
your

Z

zigzag
zoo